PARENTING TEENAGE GIRLS FOR PURPOSE

Guiding Godly Young Girls to Walk in Charisma, Character, Calling, Life Skills, and Christ-Centered Confidence

Bukky Ekine-Ogunlana

© Copyright Bukky Ekine-Ogunlana 2025 – All rights reserved.

The content contained within this book may not be reproduced, duplicated, or transmitted without direct written permission from the author or the publisher.

Under no circumstance should any blame or legal responsibility be held against the publisher, or author, for any damages, reparation, or monetary loss due to the information contained within this book. Either directly or indirectly. You are responsible for your own choices, actions, and results.

Legal Notice:

This book is copyright protected. This book is only for personal use. You cannot amend, distribute, sell, use, quote, or paraphrase any part, or the content within this book, without the consent of the author or publisher.

Disclaimer Notice:

Please note the information contained within this document is for educational and entertainment purposes only. All effort has been executed to present accurate, up-to-date, and reliable, complete information. No warranties of any kind are declared or implied. Readers acknowledge that the author is not engaging in the rendering of legal, financial, medical, or professional advice. The content within this book has been derived from various sources. Please consult a licensed professional before attempting any techniques outlined in this book

By reading this document, the reader agrees that under no circumstances is the author responsible for any losses, direct or indirect, which are incurred as a result of the use of the information contained within this document, including, but not limited to,—errors, omissions, or inaccuracies.

Published by

TCEC Publishing

TCEC House

England, Great Britain

Dedication

This book is dedicated to our three amazing children and all the beautiful children worldwide who have passed through the T.C.E.C 6-16 years program over the years. Thank you for the opportunity to serve you and invest in your colorful and bright future.

Table of Contents

Introduction: You're Not Alone in This 6

Chapter 1: Her Faith, Her Journey 9

Chapter 2: Staying Connected When Emotions Run High 14

Chapter 3: Social Media, Screens, and the Pressure to Be "Perfect" 20

Chapter 4: Nurturing Her Faith in a World of Doubt and Distraction .. 24

Chapter 5: Hearing God, Obeying God The Power of the Holy Spirit Within 27

Chapter 6: Helping Her Know Who She Is (and Whose She Is) 33

Chapter 7: Faith and Mental Health They Can Go Together 41

Chapter 8: Discovering Her Purpose 45

Chapter 9: Discipline That Builds Her Up Not Breaks 56

Chapter 10: Life Skills Every Teen Girl Needs (That School Might Not Teach) 61

Chapter 11: Looking Ahead College, Careers, and What Comes Next 71

Chapter 12: Love, Friendships, and Everything in Between 77

Chapter 13: Motherhood That Leaves a Legacy: 12 Real-Life Lessons from the Frontlines 84

Please Leave a Review! 151

Conclusion: Keep Showing Up. Keep Trusting God. 152

Heartstrings & Heaven 156

Other Books You'll Love! 189

Your Free Gift! 193

References 194

Introduction:
You're Not Alone in This

Raising a teenage daughter today can feel like keeping your balance on a rollercoaster you didn't sign up for. Social media, culture, questions about faith, identity, and what her future might hold can all be overwhelming for anyone.

But here's the thing: you don't have to figure it all out alone. This book? It's your companion — here to encourage you, give you practical tools, and remind you that with God's help, you've got this.

Together, we'll talk about what it means to raise strong, faith-filled girls in a world that changes every day.

A Real Story: Sarah & Emily
Sarah thought she and her daughter Emily were close—Bible studies, church volunteering, endless talks. Then high school hit, and everything shifted.

Emily's friends stopped texting her. TikTok was full of content that didn't align with her faith. Suddenly, she was asking tough questions Sarah didn't have answers for:

- "Why does God care who I date?"
- "What if I don't feel close to Him anymore?"
- "Is the Bible even for girls like me?"

Sarah was scared—not because Emily was questioning, but because she wasn't sure how to respond. Instead of shutting her down, Sarah simply listened. There was no preaching, no pressure—just space to talk and lots of prayers.

Slowly, Emily started opening up again. She wasn't perfect, but she was searching for something. And most importantly, she knew her mom was someone she could be honest with — no judgment, just love.

Not Every Story Starts This Way: Mark & Rachel

Mark loved Rachel fiercely and made sure she was at church every Sunday. But faith talks at home? Rarely happened.

Mark felt lost when Rachel started dating a boy who didn't share her values. By the time he spoke up, Rachel was already attached and confused. The relationship ended badly — and so did her faith.

Rachel asked, "If God cares, why did He let this happen?"

Mark realized that just showing up on Sundays wasn't enough. He wished he'd prepared her better for the hard stuff.

Here's the Truth

Raising a teenage Christian girl today is sacred—and messy—work.

The world is loud, fast, and often harsh. It can feel like everything is pushing against the quiet, steady strength your daughter is called to live out.

But she doesn't have to be perfect. She doesn't need to quote every Bible verse or have all the answers. What matters is that she knows who she is in Christ, even when it feels like everything else is shouting the opposite.

She can't do this alone. She needs you—not just as a parent but also as her guide, coach, prayer partner, and safe place when life feels unstable.

Why This Book?

Because this journey can feel lonely.

If you're overwhelmed, praying secretly, or worried you're saying too much or not enough, this book is for you.

If you feel like you're losing your little girl, or if you want to connect but don't know how — you're not alone.

We'll discuss real struggles—such as social media, dating, faith doubts, peer pressure, and identity—with practical advice and hope-filled stories that actually work today.

A Little Encouragement

You don't need to be perfect. You need to be present.

Your daughter doesn't need all your answers. She just needs to know you're walking beside her—and that Jesus is, too. Even when it's messy, even when it's quiet, even when she says she's "fine," you know she's not.

Take a deep breath. You're doing better than you think.

Let's do this together.

After reading this guide, please feel free to leave a review based on your findings and how valuable the guide was to you. I would be incredibly thankful if you could take 60 seconds to write a brief review on the platform of purchase, even if it's just a few sentences!

Chapter 1:
Her Faith, Her Journey

Teenage faith isn't like childhood faith. It's messier. More questioning. More personal.

And that's okay.

Your daughter is figuring out how to make faith her own — not just something she's told, but something she owns deep inside.

You might wonder, "How do I help her stay grounded in Christ when the world's noise is so loud?"

Here's the thing: there's no magic formula. It's not about controlling every choice or having perfect answers to every question asked. It's all about guiding her to discover a deep, unshakable sense of who she is—rooted in God's love for her, no matter what life throws her way at any point in time.

A Real Example: Jasmine's Mirror

Jasmine was 15—bright, kind, and full of life. She used to fill the room with her curiosity and easy laugh. But slowly, something began to change around her.

It started quietly—just a few extra minutes on her phone, a little more time lost scrolling through Instagram. But with every swipe, that glowing screen started whispering lies. She didn't even realize what she was believing: *"She's prettier than you." "Her life is better." "You're not enough."*

Comparison crept in like a shadow.

Jasmine stopped sharing her thoughts at the dinner table. Church became optional. Her laughter faded, and her phone became a mirror she held up to herself—a mirror that only showed her what she lacked.

It wasn't dramatic or loud. It was subtle. But the ache was real.

And like so many teenage girls, Jasmine didn't need someone to snap her out of it or lecture her about screen time. She needed someone to notice. To see past the silence. To remind her of who she was before the filters and highlight reels started shaping her worth.

She didn't need a perfect parent—just a present one. Picture after picture of flawless girls with perfect skin, trendy outfits, and lives that looked so... easy. Jasmine started to believe she wasn't enough.

Slowly, her confidence faded. She stopped going to youth group. She stopped smiling in pictures. Even getting ready for school became a battle—she would stand in front of the mirror for way too long, picking herself apart, trying to "measure up."

Church felt distant. God felt quiet. And Jasmine? She felt small.

Her parents noticed. They didn't have all the right words, but they did something powerful—they stayed close. They reminded her of who she was in God's eyes. Not filtered. Not edited. Chosen. Loved. Enough.

It wasn't instant, but things began to shift. Jasmine started journaling prayers again. She joined a small group. She deleted a few accounts that made her feel less-than and replaced them with voices that spoke truth and life.

One evening, she told her mom, "I looked in the mirror today and didn't hate what I saw."

That's the power of reminding our daughters who they are—not just what they look like. Because when they see themselves through God's eyes, the mirror starts to look a little different.

Her mom didn't yell or lecture. Instead, she sat down with Jasmine and read Psalm 139. Then she taped encouraging Bible verses on Jasmine's mirror, reminding her she was:

- Chosen (Ephesians 1:4)
- Loved (Romans 8:38–39)
- Made on purpose (Psalm 139:13–16)

It wasn't instant, but slowly, Jasmine began to believe what God had said about her more than what social media had shouted.

A Bible Story to Remember

Think about the woman at the well in John 4. She was carrying shame, trying to fill her emptiness with relationships. Jesus met her where she was without judgment.

He offered her living water, which satisfied her deep inside, not just for a moment.

"Whoever drinks the water I give them will never thirst again." (John 4:14)

Your daughter might not be standing at a well, but she's thirsty — for love, acceptance, and identity. Help her drink from the only source that truly satisfies. Jesus wants to install a well inside so that he can release living water to others.

What You Can Do Right Now

You don't need to be a Bible scholar. You need to show up and speak the truth, little by little.

Try This: "I See You" Notes

Write quick notes and hide them in her backpack, mirror, or phone charger. Stuff like:

- "You are loved — no matter what."
- "God made you strong and beautiful."
- "Don't forget who you are."

Even if she rolls her eyes, these small reminders stick.

Try a Shared Journal

Leave a notebook on her nightstand where you can write thoughts, prayers, encouragement, or even apologies. Sometimes, teens open up better in writing than in conversation.

When Silence Speaks

Rachel was a church kid but never talked much about faith at home. Her parents assumed she "got it."

Then high school happened. She dated a boy who didn't share her values, and her identity shifted to match his view of her. When the relationship ended, she walked away—not just from him but also from her faith.

It wasn't rebellion. It was confusion.

Please don't assume your daughter knows who she is. Keep reminding her. Keep showing up. Even when it seems like she's not listening — she is.

Small Things, Big Impact

- Pick one Bible verse a week to read and talk about together.
- When you correct her, focus on identity, not just behaviour:
- "That choice doesn't fit who you are. You're strong, honest, and loved."
- Celebrate her heart and growth, not just her achievements.

Questions to Think About

1. Where might your daughter be looking for identity right now?
2. Do your words remind her who she is in Christ — or just what she does?
3. What's one way you can speak life into her this week?

Thoughts

Your daughter doesn't need perfect parents. She needs parents who show up, love well, and keep pointing her back to Jesus.

She'll have questions. She'll wander. That's part of the journey.

Your job is to walk beside her — steady, patient, and full of grace.

Keep loving her, praying, and speaking the truth — even if it feels like she's not listening.

One day, those seeds will bloom.

Because when she truly knows who she is in Christ, the world won't be able to shake her.

Chapter 2:
Staying Connected When Emotions Run High

If you're raising a teenage girl, you already know the rollercoaster ride. One moment, she's curled up beside you nicely, giggling about her day—and the next, she's storming off, slamming a door, or shutting you out with silence that stings which can sometimes not be understandable.

It's intense. It's unpredictable. And let's be honest—it can feel completely exhausting.

You might find yourself wondering, *How do I reach her when she feels so far away? What happened to the little girl who used to run into my arms without hesitation?*

Here's the truth that can shift everything: her emotions aren't walls meant to keep you out—they're doors.

Yes, messy, creaky, sometimes confusing doors. But when you approach them gently—with the power of patience, grace, and a love that doesn't give up—they can open. And when they do, they lead to something powerful: deeper connection, mutual trust, and a relationship that grows stronger through every up and down.

You don't have to have all the answers. You just have to keep showing up. With love. With steady presence. With an open heart.

She may not always say it, but she still needs you—especially now.

A Biblical Example: Hannah's Quiet, Faithful Love

Think of Hannah in the Old Testament (1 Samuel 1–2). For years, she longed for a child. Her heart broke with sorrow, and her prayers poured like a river. When God finally answered with the birth of Samuel, she made a difficult promise—she would give him back to God's service. Hannah's story is a very powerful example of a mother's love and faithfulness, even in the face of challenges and distance.

Imagine Hannah stitching a petite robe for her son every year, a simple act of love and connection despite the distance (1 Samuel 2:19). She didn't control Samuel's life or force her presence; she stayed faithful, present, and loving.

When your daughter pulls away emotionally or physically, you can learn from Hannah's quiet faithfulness. You don't need to fix everything or have all the answers. Just keep showing up, loving her consistently, and trusting God to work in her heart through your prayers.

A Modern Story: The Bedroom Door

Here's Jenna's story.

After a heated argument with her 15-year-old daughter, Kayla, Jenna stood silently outside her bedroom door. Her heart pounded in her chest as she replayed the sharp words, the slammed door, and the deep ache that now sat in her stomach like a stone. She felt the sting of regret—things she wished she hadn't said, things she wanted Kayla hadn't told either.

Everything in her wanted to react. To march in, demand respect, and get to the bottom of it all. But instead, she paused. Her hand hovered near the doorknob, but she didn't turn it. Not yet.

In that quiet hallway, Jenna took a breath—and chose something different. She decided to stay present rather than force her way in. She whispered a prayer: *God, help me to meet her with grace, not control. Help me be a safe place, not a storm.*

Minutes passed. Then, from the other side of the door came the soft sound of crying. Not loud or attention-seeking—just quiet, broken sobs. And Jenna's heart softened even more.

She knocked gently. "Kayla... I'm here. I love you. When you're ready, I'm not going anywhere."

No lectures. No pressure. Just your presence, which is more valuable than you may realize.

And that moment—simple and quiet—became the beginning of healing. Not because Jenna had all the answers but because she stayed.

Instead, Jenna sat down quietly outside the door, whispered a prayer for patience, and said, "I'm here when you're ready. I love you."

After what felt like forever, Kayla cracked open the door, tear-streaked and hesitant. "Why do you still care?" she asked.

Jenna met her gaze and answered, "Because you're my daughter, nothing will change that."

That night wasn't about solving problems or having perfect words. It was about presence—showing her daughter that love remains, even in the storm.

What This Means for You, Mom and Dad

- **Pause before reacting.** Take a breath. Listen to understand, not just to respond.

- **Validate her feelings.** Saying, "I see that this is hard for you", words matter more than you might think.

- **Offer your presence first.** Sometimes, just sitting quietly beside her says more than any advice.

- **Pray together and for each other.** Invite God into the messy moments.

- **Model your emotional health.** Share your feelings and how God helps you through struggles.

Reflection and Action Steps

Remember the last time your daughter's emotions caught you off guard? How did you respond?

Try a straightforward practice this week: listen to her fully in one conversation without jumping in to fix or judge.

Pray this daily:

"Lord, help me see my daughter as You see her—fearfully and wonderfully made. Give me patience and wisdom to guide her with love."

Why This Chapter Matters

Many parents tell me they want to connect but feel powerless when emotions flare. They fear pushing too hard or stepping back too much. This chapter offers hope and practical guidance on building trust and closeness, even in the most challenging moments.

More Than Just Emotions

Let's be honest—parenting a teenage girl can feel like you're buckled into a rollercoaster with no map, no brakes, and definitely no seatbelt. One minute, she's dancing in the kitchen, laughing at her own jokes, music blaring like life is perfect. The next, she's curled up in her room behind a closed door, tears spilling over something you may never fully understand.

And there you are—caught in the middle—trying to navigate the silence, the mood swings, the slammed doors, and the rare, beautiful moments of connection that feel like sunlight breaking through the clouds.

It's exhausting. It's confusing. And on some nights—when the house is finally quiet—you wonder silently, *Am I getting any of this right?*

But here's the beautiful, often-overlooked truth: every emotional swing isn't just drama—it's a doorway. Every outburst, every breakdown, every eye-roll or tear-streaked moment—even those unexpected bursts of laughter in the middle of chaos—they're not just noise or mess. They're invitations.

Not invitations to fix her. Not to have the perfect response. But to *be there*.

To show up with open arms, not all the answers. To bring a steady presence is not a perfect solution. Because what she's really asking—underneath the storm—is, *"Are you still with me? Even now?"*

And when we choose to stay, to love without trying to control, we're speaking something sacred into her soul: *You are safe. You are seen. You are not alone.*

That's what she'll remember—not what you fixed, but how you stayed.

Because when we stop trying to control the chaos and instead lean in with compassion, we begin to reflect something sacred. We mirror the heart of God—not a God who scolds from afar, but one who draws close. Who doesn't demand perfection but offers presence. Steady. Gentle. Faithful. Always near.

And that's what your daughter needs more than anything. Not a perfect parent. Just one who stays.

That kind of love—yours—is what your daughter will remember. Even if she can't always say it. His Word reminds us that emotions aren't weaknesses—they're windows into what really matters. When you choose to listen instead of lecture, to comfort instead of correct, you show her the kind of love that transforms hearts.

You don't have to get it perfect. You just have to keep showing up with grace.

A Prayer for You

God, when my daughter's emotions feel bigger than I can handle, help me to stay steady. Teach me to listen without rushing to fix and to love her the way You love me—patiently, faithfully, and without judgment. When I don't understand her, help me hold space anyway. Remind me, Lord, that I don't have to have it all figured out. My daughter doesn't need a perfect parent—she just needs a steady one. Help me be her safe place, the kind of presence that quietly says, "You're never alone." Fill me with Your wisdom when mine runs out, and let Your peace settle over me when things feel heavy. Shape my heart to look more like Yours, full of grace and patience, no matter what the day holds. Amen.

Chapter 3:
Social Media, Screens, and the Pressure to Be "Perfect"

Your daughter is growing up in a world that feels completely different from what you knew. Instagram, TikTok, Snapchat—these aren't just apps or ways to pass the time; they're stages where she's constantly showing who she is, measured by likes, followers, and the latest trends.

This digital world can feel like a heavy weight pressing down on her—the kind you can't always see, but she feels every day. It's the constant pressure to look flawless, to be liked, to post the right picture with the perfect caption at just the right time. It's not just about being seen—it's about being approved.

And that kind of pressure doesn't disappear when she puts her phone down. It lingers. In the quiet moments. In the mirror. In the comparison that creeps in when she sees someone else's highlight reel and wonders if she'll ever be "enough."

It can stir up a swirl of emotions she may not know how to name—comparison that cuts deep, anxiety that tightens her chest, self-doubt that shadows her confidence. She might not talk about it, but she feels it.

That's why your steady presence matters so much. Not to fix it or fight against every app, but to gently remind her of what's real. To help her anchor her worth in something unchanging. To be the voice that tells her she's already deeply loved—not because of how she appears online, but because of who she is at her core. As a parent, it's natural to want to step in as the "tech police," laying down strict rules or even banning devices altogether, hoping to protect her from the stress. But more often than not, that pushes her away, making her hide her struggles or push back instead of opening up.

A Biblical Story: David and Jonathan — Friendship Without Competition

Consider David and Jonathan's friendship (1 Samuel 18-20). Jonathan was the prince, next in line for the throne, while David was the up-and-coming hero, seen by many as a threat. But rather than compete or let jealousy take hold, Jonathan chose to stand by David—protecting his name, cheering him on, and encouraging him to be his true self. Their bond wasn't about rivalry but loyalty, trust, and genuine love.

Your daughter needs the same kind of support: a safe space where she can be herself—unfiltered, imperfect, and loved just as she is. It is not a competition to be "better" or "more liked," but a relationship built on genuine encouragement and loyalty.

A Modern-Day Story: The Deleted Post

One night, Rachel noticed her 14-year-old daughter Ava scrolling on her phone with a frown, deleting a photo she'd just posted.

Rachel gently asked, "Are you okay?"

Ava shrugged, "I didn't like how I looked. Not many people liked it anyway. What's the point?"

Instead of lecturing, Rachel quietly said, "I get that. I've felt that way too. But your worth isn't measured by likes or followers. I love who you are when no one's watching—that girl is incredible."

Ava's tears spoke louder than words. "You have to say that — you're my mom."

Rachel smiled, "I mean it, always."

That night didn't solve everything, but it planted a seed—a reminder that her value isn't something she can earn online; it's something she already carries inside.

What You Can Do: Guiding Without Controlling

- **Set boundaries together.** Please talk with your daughter about screen time limits and why they matter. Make it a partnership, not a punishment.

- **Help her curate her feed.** Encourage unfollowing accounts that spark comparison or anxiety. Teach her to follow voices that build her up.

- **Create tech-free zones.** Family dinners, car rides, or before bed — these moments foster real connection and calm.

- **Model healthy habits.** Show how you balance your screen time and put devices down to be present.

- **Speak her identity often.** Remind her that she's chosen, loved, and enough — no filter needed.

- **Lead with curiosity, not fear.** Ask what she enjoys online and what stresses her, and listen openly.

Why This Matters
Social media and screens aren't the enemy. Silence or punishment around them can leave your daughter feeling alone in her struggles. What she needs is your steady love, your listening ear, and your gentle guidance.

You are her safe harbour in a noisy, demanding world.

A Prayer for You
God, this world is loud, and my daughter's heart is tender. Help me speak the truth that cuts through the noise. When she forgets her worth, remind her through me—or whatever You choose. Give me wisdom, grace, and words at the right time. And when words fail, let my presence be enough. Amen.

Chapter 4:
Nurturing Her Faith in a World of Doubt and Distraction

Adolescence isn't just about growing taller or changing physically; it's also about developing internally, emotionally and mentally. It's a time when your daughter starts wrestling with big questions: *Who am I? Why am I here? What do I believe?*

As a parent, especially a Christian parent, it can be unsettling to hear your daughter question the faith you've prayed over and nurtured. You might worry: Is she losing her way? But here's the truth—doubt is a normal part of the journey. It doesn't mean she's failing. Often, it means she's beginning to make faith her own in a real and meaningful way.

A Biblical Inspiration: Thomas the Disciple
Remember Thomas in John 20:24-29? When the other disciples told him Jesus had risen, he said, "I need to see it for myself." Jesus didn't scold him or call him faithless. Instead, Jesus met Thomas right where he was—doubts and all—and gently gave him the proof he needed.

This story reminds us that Jesus welcomes questions and doubts. Your daughter's faith journey might look similar: one of seeking, wondering, and wrestling before she fully embraces faith as her own.

A Real-Life Story: Rachel's Journey

Rachel grew up in church, learned verses by heart, and faithfully attended youth group. But in high school, as her friends and the world around her changed, so did her questions. Faith began to feel like a list of rules rather than a relationship, and she pulled away.

Instead of pushing her, Rachel's parents made space for honest conversations at the dinner table. They shared their struggles and doubts without judgment. Rachel began journaling her questions and eventually attended a faith-based camp. One evening during worship, she experienced God in a way that profoundly changed her life. Her doubts didn't vanish in an instant—but something real began to grow deep inside. Her faith, once borrowed and distant, slowly became her own. It wasn't perfect or polished, but it was personal. Each step she took—asking questions, choosing to trust, learning to listen—wove her heart closer to God. It wasn't about having it all figured out. It was about finally knowing *why* she believed and *who* she belonged to.

A Modern-Day Reality

You've probably heard the term' faith deconstruction' tossed around—especially for young people. And while it might sound alarming initially, it's not always a sign that your daughter is walking away from her faith. In fact, for many teens, it's a positive step in their faith journey, a sign of growth and maturity.

They're not necessarily rejecting God—they're sifting through what they've been taught all along, asking hard questions, and trying to figure out what's real and just tradition. It's less about tearing everything down and more about rebuilding something honest and personal. They want a faith that holds up in real life—not just on Sunday mornings but all their lives.

As a parent, your role is crucial at this time. It's not to panic or preach louder, not at all. It's to create a safe space for her to unfold her questions, hold space for her doubts, and trust that God is big enough for every bit of her wrestling. Because often, it's through the messiness of questioning that genuine, unshakable faith begins to take root.

What You Can Do: Try This

- **Faith Q&A Nights:** Once a month, invite your daughter to write down any questions about God or faith—even anonymously if she wants. Then, discuss them together openly and gently.

- **Share Your Journey:** Be honest about times when God felt distant or you struggled. Vulnerability creates connection.

- **Encourage Personal Habits:** Help her find a Bible reading plan, start a prayer journal, or discover worship music that moves her heart.

- **Support Her Encounters:** Take her to youth retreats, concerts, or workshops where she can experience faith for herself, not just inherit it.

Chapter 5:
Hearing God, Obeying God
The Power of the Holy Spirit Within

"It was just a regular Sunday — nothing out of the ordinary. But for Emma, it marked the start of something a new. Her dad noticed a change in her, something subtle but real, and he didn't want to miss it. When she came downstairs that morning, asking how to hear God's voice, he knew this was one of those moments that mattered. He slowed down, ready to really listen."

"Sit," he said warmly, patting the couch. "Let's talk."

The Conversation That Changed Everything

Her father began not with rules but with a story—his own. Years ago, he had learned that Jesus doesn't just want our attendance in church or a moral checklist; He wants our hearts. He wants **a relationship**. And a relationship, he emphasized, requires something powerful: **obedience**.

He pointed to **Acts 5:32**: *"We are witnesses of these things, and so is the Holy Spirit, whom God has given to those who obey him."* "He explained that this verse shows how the Holy Spirit can truly change us — helping us grow, transform, and become more of who we're meant to be."

He looked her in the eye: "God becomes powerful in your life not just because you believe, but because you obey. His Spirit lives in you — and He wants to lead you."

A Friend Named Lillian

Emma's journey deepened when she introduced her friend Lillian to their weekly Bible study group. Lillian was nothing like the girls at church—bold, with piercings and tattoos and a guarded heart. She'd been bounced around foster homes, used to being tough to survive.

But the Word of God has a way of cutting through walls. One evening, during a simple study on grace, Lillian sat silently. Her fists clenched. Then, tears.

"I didn't know I needed saving," she whispered. "But I do."

That night, something holy happened. Lillian prayed — not a fancy prayer, just raw and honest. She confessed, "I've messed up. But if Jesus can save me, I want Him."

She believed. The weight lifted.

Over the following days, she wrestled with doubts. Was she saved? Could someone like a holy God love her? But a deep knowing began to settle in. She read in John 6:37, *"Whoever comes to me I will never cast out."* That verse became her anchor.

The Voice Within

Soon after, Lillian started to hear something she couldn't explain — a still, small voice. One morning, she looked in the mirror and sensed the Spirit asking, *"Can you remove the ring in your nose?"*

Not in shame. Not because someone told her to. But because a **new voice** was shaping her.

She'd later tell Emma, "I realized the way I dressed, the music I used to love, even the way I talked — a different spirit inspired all of it. But now, I want the Holy Spirit to own me. I want Him to shape me."

So, step by step, she obeyed. The ring came out. The language softened. The music shifted. Her style changed, not to fit in at church — but to reflect the **new voice** that now ruled her heart.

It wasn't easy. There were tears. Confusion. Lonely moments. But always — peace, a peace that surpasses all understanding and reassures us that we are on the right path.

Inner Life: The Silent Battle

Both Emma and Lillian began to understand that **obedience isn't about legalism**. It's about **intimacy**.

Obedience says, "I trust You more than I trust myself." It's how we build the infrastructure for Christ to live in us — not just as an idea but as a **governing Presence**.

Emma learned this one day when insulted by a classmate in front of a crowd. Her first instinct? Snap back. Defend herself. But the Holy Spirit nudged her in that split second: *"Be quiet. You're mine."*

She swallowed hard. Walked away. Later, she cried — not out of shame, but out of growth.

"I chose obedience," she told her dad. "And I think God trusted me with that moment."

He smiled. "That's maturity. That's Jesus being powerful in your life."

When the Spirit Speaks

Lillian once described the Holy Spirit like this: *"It's like there's someone in my chest now. I sense the movement. When I'm about to do something off, I feel it — like a quiet sadness or a whisper saying, 'Don't go there.'"* This is the Holy Spirit, our constant companion, guiding us in our decisions and actions.

And when she obeys? *"It's like heaven claps. I don't hear it with my ears, but I feel it in my soul."*

Jesus said in **John 10:27**, *"My sheep hear my voice, and I know them, and they follow me."* That voice is authentic. And the more you listen, the clearer it becomes.

He doesn't shout. He **commands through love** — like a good Father.

Sometimes, those commandments are personal:
- Don't respond to that DM.
- Turn off that song.
- Apologize first.
- Don't buy that — it's not worth your peace.

These aren't rules to restrict — they're boundaries to **protect**. Like a good shepherd, He leads us into green pastures and away from wolves.

When You're Chosen, You'll Be Commanded

Lillian asked Emma, "How do you know if you're chosen?"

Emma smiled. "Because He's giving you commandments."

Every chosen one is a **commanded one**. God won't leave you in confusion if you stay close. He'll tell you how to treat people, how to handle money, how to speak, and how to live.

That's how you know He's near.

You are not a stray. You are known.

And His commandments? They're not burdens. They're boundaries of love.

Reflection Questions
1. Do I recognize the Holy Spirit as someone who wants to lead me?
2. Have I responded to His voice, even when it's uncomfortable?
3. What areas of my life is the Spirit asking me to surrender?
4. Am I raising my daughter to value obedience as the path to spiritual power?

A Prayer
"Father, thank You for the gift of the Holy Spirit. Please help me and my daughter walk in obedience, even when it's hard. Let us hear Your voice clearly and follow without hesitation. Teach us to trust You, to obey You, and to reflect Your holiness in our everyday choices. In Jesus' name, Amen."

Father-Daughter Conversation Guide
- **Ask her:**
    - What do you think God is saying to you these days?
    - Is there something He's asking you to give up or change?
    - How can I help you listen to Him?
- **Say to her:**
    - I'm not here to police you. I want to walk with you.

- I believe you can hear God.

- Obedience isn't about being perfect — it's about being willing.

Let the Holy Spirit be the loudest voice in your home. That's where true power lies.

Chapter 6:
Helping Her Know Who She Is (and Whose She Is)

Let's be real—the world is always shouting at your daughter about who she should be. Social media is full of flawless selfies, perfect bodies, and filtered lives. Her friends might be sending mixed messages, and everywhere she looks, ads tell her what's "in" or "out," who's cool and who's not. It makes any young girl feel confused, pressured, or exhausted.

But here's a rock-solid truth you can cling to—and pass on to her:

Her identity is already set, fully defined by the One who made her. God knows her better than anyone ever will. He loves her not for what she looks or does but simply because she's His daughter.

When your daughter truly understands *who* she is, she gains quiet strength. That strength that helps her say "No" to the voice that says she's not enough and "Yes" to the truth that she's loved and chosen just as she is.

The Bible's Take on Who She Is

Psalm 139:14 says, *"I praise you because I am fearfully and wonderfully made."* Ephesians 2:10 reminds us, *"We are God's handiwork, created in Christ Jesus to do good works."* These aren't just pretty words for a Sunday school poster—they're the foundation for how your daughter can see herself every day.

Moses and His Mom: Knowing Who You Are, No Matter Where You Are

Here's a story I love: Moses. His mom, Jochebed, ensured he knew from the beginning that he wasn't just any boy. She reminded him he was a Hebrew—a child of God's people—even though he was raised in Pharaoh's palace surrounded by wealth and luxury.

Think about that: Moses grew up with all the riches, education, and temptations anyone could want. But because he *knew* who he was, he didn't get lost in it all. He stood firm, even in the middle of a palace full of distractions.

Today, your daughter is growing up in a world of distractions and pressures like that palace. If she knows her identity—who God says she is—she'll have the courage to stand firm no matter what comes her way.

The Spiritual Womb: Where Prayer Brings God's Plans to Life

Just like your daughter's body has a womb designed to bring new life into the world, she also has a *spiritual womb*. This is where her prayers live—where her hopes, dreams, and even doubts can grow and take shape.

This spiritual womb isn't just a nice idea. It's where God plants His purposes for her life. When she prays with faith, she's inviting God to birth those dreams and plans into reality.

The Daughters of Zelophehad: Bold Women Who Prayed and Acted

In the Bible, the daughters of Zelophehad (Numbers 27:1-7) lost their father and had no brothers to inherit his land. Instead of giving up, they prayed, trusted God, and boldly stood up to claim what was rightfully theirs.

Their story shows your daughter that prayer isn't passive or quiet. It's active and influential—how we bring God's justice and purpose into the world.

Jesus' Disciples: "Teach Us to Pray"
Here's a little-known fact: when Jesus' disciples came to Him, they didn't ask, "Teach us how to preach" or "Teach us to perform miracles." They asked, *"Teach us how to pray."*

Why? Because they saw that when they tried to fix things on their own, they couldn't. But when Jesus prayed, things changed. Healing happened. Hearts were moved. That's the power of prayer.

This is a lesson your daughter can learn from you—that prayer is her most powerful tool. It's how she partners with God to bring change, healing, and purpose into her life and those around her.

Obeying from the Heart: Where Love Meets Action
One evening, Dad sat down with his daughter, Emma. She'd been trying to read the Bible—marking the promises in green and the commandments in blue like he had taught her. But the words still felt distant, like a puzzle she couldn't solve.

"Dad," Emma said quietly, "sometimes I don't get it when I read the Bible. I try, but it feels too much, so I stop."

Dad smiled kindly. "I understand, Emma. You know, Obedience is an act—not just a wish or something we do because someone told us to. It's something we choose from the heart. And that's often where true understanding starts to grow."

Emma tilted her head, a little confused. "What do you mean? Isn't obeying just... doing the right thing?"

Her dad smiled gently. "Sometimes we think Obedience means just following the rules, like checking a box. But it's deeper than that. Real Obedience isn't just about behaviour—it's about the heart behind it. Something shifts when we choose to obey God from a place of love and trust, not just duty or fear. His truth starts to make sense. His voice becomes clearer. And we begin to understand—not just what He's asking, but why."

Emma sat quietly for a moment. "So it's kind of like... taking a step even when you don't see the whole staircase?"

"Exactly," her dad nodded. "And as you take those steps, God meets you there. Obedience opens the door for a relationship, and a relationship brings revelation."

"Do you remember when you were little, and I used to make you brush your teeth—even when you didn't understand why and you didn't want to? At that age, trying to explain cavities or hygiene wouldn't have made any sense to you. But I still made you do it because I knew it was important. And now, brushing your teeth twice a day is second nature to you—and you understand why it's essential.

That's a bit like how it works with God's Word, too. There are times when we won't fully understand what He's asking of us or why. But that doesn't mean we should wait to obey. Understanding often comes *after* obedience.

Jesus even says in John 7:17, 'If anyone chooses to do God's will, he will find out whether my teaching comes from God or whether I speak on my own.' In other words, when we start with the decision to obey, clarity and understanding begin to follow. Just like you eventually understood the importance of brushing your teeth, we'll come to understand God's wisdom more and more—if we're willing to trust and follow Him first."

That means you don't have to understand everything right away. But the understanding will come when you choose to obey and start with that decision."

Emma nodded slowly. "So I must obey first, even if I don't get it yet?"

"Exactly." Dad's eyes softened. "I know you've been following me and the family to church and reading the Bible because it was expected of you. But maybe it never really touched your heart. That's why it felt like a drag—it wasn't personal. It was just something you were doing because you had to."

Emma looked down, thinking. "Yeah, that sounds like me."

"But when you begin to obey from your heart, something changes. You start to feel convicted—like your soul is being cleaned out. You begin to own your decision to follow Jesus, not just because I say so, but because you want to."

Emma's eyes brightened a little. "That sounds different. Has that happened to you?"

Dad nodded. "It has. When that happened to me, my heart changed. My desires started to shift. The things I used to want, like spending endless hours on my phone or watching random shows, didn't interest me as much anymore. Instead, God began to put new desires in me—the desire to pray, help others, and live out what He wants for me."

Emma smiled, hopeful. "I want that too."

"Good," Dad said. "When God's Word cleanses your heart like that, it changes your taste buds—so to speak. Suddenly, you want different things, better things. Your screen time goes down because you want to spend time with God and people. You start living out His desires every day."

Emma took a deep breath. "But obeying all the commandments still feels like a lot."

Dad chuckled softly, his eyes were kind. "It *is* a lot. But think of it like this—imagine a pomegranate. Did you know it has around 613 seeds packed with nutrients that help your body stay strong and healthy? The Old Testament has about 613 commandments, too. Following them is like feeding your spirit—each nourishing a different part of your soul, helping you grow strong, whole, and connected to God."

He paused, then added gently, "But Jesus helped us see the heart of it all. In the New Testament, He summed up all those commandments into two: Love God with all your heart, and love your neighbour as yourself. Everything else flows from that. So instead of trying to carry 613 separate rules, think of love as the root—and the commandments as the fruit it bears."

Emma smiled. "That's a cool way to think about it."

"And obeying God's commands is like having a strong backbone,"

Dad continued. "Your skeleton holds you up when life's storms come. Without that backbone, you're like a worm on the ground—easy to crush, no strength to stand."

Emma's face lit up. "I want to be strong like that."

Dad looked at her warmly. "Many people say they love God, but God only recognizes those who obey His written Word and listen to His prompting in their hearts. Jesus said in John 14:21, 'Whoever has my commands and keeps them is the one who loves me.' And in Matthew 4:4, He reminds us, 'Man shall not live by bread alone, but by every word that comes from the mouth of God.' Loving God means living out what He tells us daily—not just saying it."

Emma nodded with quiet determination. "I want to obey with my heart, not just follow the rules."

"That's the best place to start," Dad said proudly. "I believe you'll live a wholesome, strong life because of it. And I'll be here to help you every step of the way."

Hannah's Story: A Girl Who Learned to Pray Boldly

Take Hannah, a quiet girl from a small town. She often felt invisible, but her mom taught her to pray intentionally—treating her prayers like seeds planted in that spiritual womb.

Slowly but surely, Hannah's prayers became bold actions. She started mentoring younger girls at church and became a source of inspiration in her community.

Mary's Journey: From Doubt to Confidence

Mary was your typical teenager—anxious, unsure, and overshadowed by her louder, more confident friends. But her parents made it a habit of speaking God's truth over her daily and encouraged her to write down what God said about her.

Over time, Mary's confidence grew—not because she was like everyone else, but because she saw herself through God's eyes. This helped her stand firm when peer pressure tried to pull her in other directions.

Peer Pressure: Saying No When It's Hard

Peer pressure is tough—there's no doubt about it. But your daughter can learn to say "No" with grace and confidence.

Look at Sara: Invited to a party that clashed with her faith, she chose church instead. It wasn't easy, but she was anchored in who she was.

Proverbs 13:20 says, *"Whoever walks with the wise becomes wise."* Help your daughter surround herself with friends who lift her and celebrate the unique gifts God has given her.

What You Can Do as a Parent

- Speak God's truth over her every day. Use verses like Ephesians 2:10 and Romans 8:38-39 as powerful reminders of her worth.

- Encourage her to journal or pray about who God says she is. Ask her, "Who am I in God's eyes?"

- Teach her about her spiritual womb—the power of prayer to birth God's plans—and encourage her to pray with hope and expectation.

- Share stories like Moses, his mom, and Jesus' disciples to show how prayer and identity shape our lives.

- Model your faith and confidence in Christ. Your daughter will learn a great deal by watching you live your faith out loud.

- Read and talk about Scripture together regularly. Let God's Word be the solid ground beneath her feet.

- Help her find and build friendships that encourage faith and celebrate her true self.

Your daughter is fearfully and wonderfully made. God deeply loves her and carries inside her a spiritual womb where amazing purposes are growing—waiting to be prayed into life. With your love, support, and prayers, she will step boldly into the incredible woman God created her to be.

Chapter 7:
Faith and Mental Health
They Can Go Together

Mental health struggles are very real for today's teens, and faith doesn't exclude those challenges—it can be the anchor through anxiety, sadness, and stress. Many parents feel unsure of how to support their daughters through emotional ups and downs, especially when faith feels distant or complicated.

Here's the good news: Your daughter's faith cannot only coexist with mental health challenges, but it can also be a powerful tool in leading her towards hope, healing, and resilience.

Biblical Foundation: The Peace That Surpasses Understanding

Philippians 4:6-7 says, *"Do not be anxious about anything... And the peace of God, which transcends all understanding, will guard your hearts and minds in Christ Jesus."* This promise isn't just for grown-ups with jobs, bills, and responsibilities—it's for your daughter, too. It's a lifeline she can hold onto when life feels like too much.

When the friend group shifts without warning. When she doesn't make the team. When her heart is racing before a big test, or she's lying in bed scrolling through a feed that makes her feel like she'll never measure up.

God's promise—that He is with her, that He sees her, that He cares—isn't something she has to wait to grow into. It's for *right now*. She can return to the steady truth when everything else feels shaky.

"As a parent, you have a special opportunity to help these truths take root in your daughter's heart. It's not just about saying the right things — it's about showing them through how you show up, how you listen, and how you love her, no matter what."

A Positive Story: Leah's Journey Through Anxiety

Leah was once a joyful, outgoing teen, but as anxiety took hold, she began pulling away from family, friends, and faith. Her mom noticed the change and gently asked how Leah was doing. Together, they prayed and sought professional support.

Leah learned to trust God's promises of peace and combined that with healthy habits—good sleep, exercise, and openness about her feelings. Slowly, hope and joy returned. Her faith became a source of strength, not guilt or shame.

What You Can Do: Supporting Mental Health with Faith

- **Promote healthy routines.** More than many realize, regular sleep, physical activity, and balanced nutrition affect mood and resilience.

- **Share your own coping strategies with your daughter.** Your example in prayer, journaling, or seeking advice from trusted friends can be a powerful tool in her mental health journey. **Focus on solutions, not just problems.** Teach your daughter to identify what helps her feel better and build those habits.

- **Normalize failure and growth.** Remind her that setbacks are part of learning and that God's grace covers every stumble.

- **Pray together consistently.** Invite God into her daily struggles and victories.

A Negative Story: When Mental Health Is Ignored

Jake's daughter Emma started struggling quietly but was told to "just pray more" and "have stronger faith." Without open conversation or support, her anxiety worsened. She felt isolated and ashamed. Eventually, with counselling and faith combined, Emma began healing, but the delay was painful for the whole family.

Why This Matters

Faith isn't a quick fix or a magic wand for mental health. But when nurtured alongside professional care and healthy habits, faith provides hope, peace, and a loving foundation to help your daughter navigate life's storms.

Remember: Your lovely daughter is not a project to fix or a puzzle to solve—she is a masterpiece, hand-crafted by God, woven with purpose and beauty from the inside out. Likes, followers, grades, or trends do not define her. She's characterized by a love that never changes.

And when you gently help her uncover that truth—when you remind her, over and over, that her worth isn't up for debate—you're giving her something the world can't take away. You're not just teaching her how to get through hard days or resist the pressure to be someone she's not. You're anchoring her in a steady truth even when everything else feels uncertain.

You're helping her build a life rooted in something more profound than appearance, performance, or popularity—a life rooted in love—the kind of love that sees her, knows her, and calls her worthy, always.

When you remind her that she's more than her reflection, her likes, or her grades... that she is loved, chosen, and created on purpose by a God who doesn't change... you're giving her a foundation the world can't crack.

And as she begins to believe that—really believe it—she'll start to stand taller. Not because everything is perfect but because she knows who she is... and who she is.

Chapter 8:
Discovering Her Purpose

Helping Your Daughter Find Meaning, Direction, and God's Plan

Why Finding Purpose Matters—For Her and You

Hey there, Mom and Dad,

Watching your daughter grow up is a journey filled with joy and fulfillment. You want so much for her—to be happy and confident and to know who she is. "Let's be honest — there are times when it feels like she's just drifting, trying to find her way without a map. like Abraham had to leave his country without a map of where he his going. And maybe, if you're honest, you're not always sure how to help her, either. But that's okay. This is a journey of discovery for both of you. And there's real joy in walking it with her, step by step."

That's why helping her discover her purpose—her God-given reason for being—is one of the best things you can do. Knowing why she's here gives her life direction, hope, and the strength to face anything.

But this isn't about pushing her or forcing a plan. It's about gently guiding her to listen to God's voice, dream with faith, and take steps—even small ones—that build her future. Remember, patience and love are crucial in this process, and they will guide you as much as they guide her. When God speaks with your daughter, His voice will reveal His purpose.

Six Daughters, Six Journeys: Helping Your Daughter Discover Her God-Given Purpose

"For we are God's masterpiece, created in Christ Jesus to do good works, which God prepared us to do." — **Ephesians 2:10**

Every girl is born with a holy whisper tucked inside her—a hint of destiny that does not always shout but always stirs. Some discover it early; others stumble upon it in heartache or obscurity. However, every daughter has a purpose. And so do you—as her parent, guardian, or guide.

Here are six real, honest, sometimes messy stories of girls who found their God-given purpose. Paired with the stories of biblical women, they remind us that what God did then, He still does now.

1. Emily, the Worship Leader

Biblical Parallel: Miriam – The Song Leader After the Storm (Exodus 15:20–21)

Emily was not the loudest girl in the room. She would hide behind her lengthy hair, blush when asked to speak and hum when anxious. However, everything changed at her church's food pantry. As she stocked shelves, her humming turned into singing. It was not long before someone heard her.

Her gift? A voice not just to sing but to *heal*.

Like Miriam, who led the people of Israel in song after they crossed the Red Sea, Emily's purpose bloomed in quiet, faithful places first. She was not chasing a spotlight—she was chasing God.

Parent Reflection: Does your daughter light up when worship music plays? Please pay attention to what she does when no one is watching.

- **Raw Gift**: Soft voice, deep sensitivity to others

- **Training**: Singing at home, YouTube, unpaid worship sets
- **Painful Process**: Stage fright, messing up lyrics in public
- **Dark Time**: Felt humiliated and considered quitting
- **Encouragements**:
    - *Psalm 40:3* — "He put a new song in my mouth..."
    - Mentor: "It is not about hitting every note—it is about bringing heaven down."
    - Mom: "Your voice may be soft, but it breaks chains."

2. Sophia the Mentor

Biblical Parallel: Naomi – The Gentle Guide to Legacy (Ruth 1–4)
Sophia never felt "special." She did not shine in sports and did not dominate classrooms. However, she *felt* deeply. She noticed who was left out. She remembered birthdays. She quietly sat with others in pain.

At youth group, she was asked to help younger girls. One small yes turned into lifelong mentorship.

Like Naomi, who thought her life was over but ended up guiding Ruth into destiny, Sophia discovered her purpose not by being the star—but by standing beside one.

Parent Reflection: If your daughter is a quiet feeler, do not mistake that for weakness. She may be someone else's anchor.

- **Raw Gift**: Deep empathy and emotional insight
- **Training**: Church counselling, informal coaching, unpaid roles

- **Painful Process**: Thought her gifts were not valuable
- **Dark Time**: Battled depression, felt invisible
- **Encouragements**:
    - *Isaiah 42:3* — "A bruised reed He will not break..."
    - Youth leader: "You are not loud, but people *lean in* when you speak."
    - Dad: "You are not the background—you are the bridge."

3. Leah the Writer

Biblical Parallel: Hannah – The Woman Who Poured Her Heart and Changed a Generation (1 Samuel 1–2)
Leah always had a notebook nearby. She wrote through joy, pain, and confusion. It was how she processed the world. No one noticed until she published a blog post about her spiritual struggles. It went viral—not for fame, but because it spoke healing.

Like Hannah, who cried out in silent grief and gave the world a prophet, Leah's raw honesty became holy.

Parent Reflection: What does your daughter reach for in times of confusion? That is often the tool God will use.

- **Raw Gift**: Expressive writing since childhood
- **Training**: School essays, blogs, poetry nights
- **Painful Process**: Rejection from publishers
- **Dark Time**: Cyberbullying made her stop writing

- **Encouragements**:
    - *Habakkuk 2:2* — "Write the vision and make it plain..."
    - Teacher: "Your words are a balm."
    - Mom: "Your pen is a sword—do not lay it down when bleeding."

4. Zoe the Midwife

Biblical Parallel: Shiphrah & Puah – The Midwives Who Defied Fear (Exodus 1:15–21)

Zoe loved babies long before she knew what midwifery was. She would swaddle dolls in tea towels and pretend to deliver life. However, real life was not pretended—she failed her first anatomy exam. She cried. She questioned God. However, she pressed in—and realized this was more than medicine. It was ministry.

Like the Hebrew midwives who risked everything to preserve the next generation, Zoe now helps usher in life with compassion and courage.

Parent Reflection: Nurturing instincts are not childish games—they may be holy whispers.

- **Raw Gift**: Nurturing, attentive care
- **Training**: Nursing school (paid), volunteering (unpaid)
- **Painful Process**: Academic failure, emotional exhaustion
- **Dark Time**: Held a grieving mother; questioned her strength
- **Encouragements**:

- *Isaiah 66:9* — "Do I bring to the moment of birth and not deliver?"
- Mentor: "You bring calm into chaos."
- Aunt: "You do not just help life enter—you protect its passage."

5. Kayla, the Project Manager

Biblical Parallel: Nehemiah – The Quiet Builder Who Held Everything Together (Nehemiah 1–6)
Kayla wasn't flashy, but she got things done. At 10, she made lists, managed her mom's birthday party at 12, and led church events at 15. She loved celebrating others but often felt unseen herself.

Like Nehemiah, who built walls with one hand and held a sword with the other, Kayla was a quiet warrior—an orchestrator of order in a chaotic world.

Parent Reflection: If your daughter thrives in organization, responsibility, and teamwork, she walks purposefully.

- **Raw Gift**: Organizing and caring for groups
- **Training**: Unpaid events, church teams, management course
- **Painful Process**: Burnout, feeling used
- **Dark Time**: Questioned her significance
- **Encouragements**:
  - *Proverbs 31:27* — "She watches over the affairs of her household..."

- o   Mentor: "You are not just efficient. You are essential."
- o   Dad: "You are the oil in the engine."

6. Hannah the Judge

Biblical Parallel: Deborah – The Judge, Prophetess, and Courageous Mother of Israel (Judges 4–5)

Hannah argued about injustice before she could spell it. When she read about Deborah in Judges, her heart leapt. She saw herself as a woman of strength, wisdom, and holy boldness. That vision carried her through law school—even when she failed her entrance exam the first time.

Now, as a judge, Hannah sees her courtroom as sacred ground.

Parent Reflection: Introduce your daughter to the Deborahs of Scripture. Sometimes, girls need to *see* a mirror to recognize their fire.

- **Raw Gift**: Passionate speech, justice sensitivity
- **Training**: Law school (paid), unpaid legal clinics, spiritual mentorship
- **Painful Process**: Academic failure, spiritual fear
- **Dark Time**: Felt too "different" in her field
- **Encouragements**:
  - o   *Judges 4:14* — "Up! This is the day..."
  - o   Professor: "Your voice is what justice sounds like."
  - o   Mom: "You are Deborah's daughter."

Word to Parents

None of these daughters woke up perfect. Their purpose was messy, raw, and slow-growing. However, God had planted seeds long before they knew what to call them. Moreover, He placed **you** beside them to water those seeds.

The purpose is not found. It is formed—slowly, through tears and triumphs.

How to Walk With Her:
- **Pray with her**, not just for her
- **Speak life** into patterns you see
- **Celebrate obedience** more than outcomes
- **Give space for failure**—without fear
- **Use Scripture** as a mirror and a map
- **Show her she is already becoming**, not waiting

What Parents Want (But Don't Always Find)

From talking with parents at parents' evenings and counselling, I've learned something important: parents want more than ideas. They want fundamental, practical tools.

- How do I help her set goals she can reach?
- How can she serve others without feeling overwhelmed?
- What if she doesn't know what she wants yet?
- How do I walk beside her without taking control?
- What if she stumbles or makes mistakes?

If these questions sound familiar, you're in the right place.

Goal Setting: Dreaming with God

Setting goals sounds fancy, but it's about helping her write down what she hopes for—big and small—while keeping God at the centre.

You can help her by:

- **Starting with prayer:** "God, what dreams do You have for me?"

- **Journaling:** Write goals like "learn a new skill" or "be kind to everyone I meet."

- **Breaking big dreams into steps:** If she wants to sing at church, maybe she can start by practising or joining the choir.

- **Being flexible:** God's timing isn't ours, and it's okay if plans change.

Serving Others: Finding Purpose Through Action

The purpose isn't just a thought; she lives by loving others. Service helps her see beyond her very self and discover gifts she didn't even know she had.

Take Emily's story. She was quiet and unsure, often blending into the background like a shadow. But everything changed when she began volunteering at the local food bank. Little by little, the light started coming back. Something quiet and beautiful grew inside her as she showed up to serve others—a deep, steady joy. It wasn't loud or flashy, but it filled her with a sense of purpose that reached places in her heart she didn't even know you were waiting to be awakened. "Before long, she was up there leading worship — her voice growing more confident with every song. That one brave step she took? It turned out to be the beginning. God used it, gently building her confidence and slowly unfolding the unique path He had just for her."

Biblical Role Models to Inspire Her

The Bible is full of stories about young women just like your daughter:
- **Esther** found the courage to stand up for her people.
- **Mary** trusted God's plan even when it was scary.
- **Deborah** was a strong leader who guided her nation.

These stories aren't just history—they're life lessons that show how God's plan often starts small but grows into something beautiful.

What If She's Struggling?

Sometimes, your daughter might feel lost, like Sophia, who felt pressured to have it all figured out and became stressed and distant from God.

That's okay. What she needs most is space, patience, and love. Remind her—and yourself—that finding purpose is a journey, not a race.

What to Focus On (And What to Skip)

Focus on:
- Easy, doable steps for goal setting and serving others.
- Real stories with ups and downs she can relate to.
- Bible examples connected to her everyday life.
- Questions you can talk through together.
- Encouragement to be patient and trust God's timing.

Skip:
- Overly complicated theories.
- Pressure to be perfect.
- One-size-fits-all "rules."
- Anything too abstract or complex to apply.

How You Can Support Her
- **Listen more than talk.** Sometimes, she needs you to hear her.
- **Celebrate the small wins.** Every step forward counts.
- **Show her by example.** Let her see you serving and living your purpose.
- **Pray with her and for her.** Make this a team effort.

Questions to Spark Conversation
- What makes you feel alive and excited?
- Who do you admire and why?
- What small things can you do today that bring you closer to God's plan?
- How can I help you figure this out?

Thought

Your daughter's purpose is like a seed planted deep inside her—sometimes hidden but ready to grow with love, care, and faith. Your steady support and prayerful guidance are the sunlight and water to help her bloom into the woman God created her to be.

Chapter 9:
Discipline That Builds Her Up
Not Breaks

Let's be real—discipline is complex. Some days, it feels like a tug-of-war you never signed up for really and did not know about. The eye rolls, pushback, and tears can wear you down. But what if discipline wasn't about power or control at all? What if it was about guiding her gently, standing beside her when everything feels confusing, and helping her grow into the strong, grounded woman God created her to be? What if, at its core, it was one of the most loving, life-giving things you could offer her? A way of saying: "I care too much to let you settle for less than who you're meant to be." Understanding this purpose can empower you, giving you a sense of control and confidence in your parenting journey.

"When you set boundaries with love — with kindness, consistency, and clear expectations — you're doing more than just correcting behaviour. You're creating a sense of peace in your home and helping your daughter feel secure and confident deep down.

Parenting a teenage girl these days? It can feel a lot like trying to hold onto a kite in the middle of a storm — wild, unpredictable, and sometimes exhausting. But your steady hand matters more than you think. "There's social media pressure, confusing messages about who she's supposed to be, and a culture that often glorifies rebellion. But you're still standing firm, balancing truth with grace, discipline with love. That takes courage.

Real-Life Moment: Rachel and Naomi

Rachel noticed that her 15-year-old daughter, Naomi, was spending time editing her photos to look thinner and more "Instagram-perfect." Instead of losing her temper or telling Naomi off, Rachel did something different.

She softly asked, "Can I ask why you needed to change your appearance?"

Naomi confessed, "Because the girls who look like that get the most likes."

Rachel didn't lecture her. She opened the Bible to Psalm 139 and read aloud:

"I praise You because I am fearfully and wonderfully made."

They prayed together and agreed Naomi would take a break from social media—not as a punishment, but to refresh her heart. Rachel gave Naomi a journal called *Who God Says I Am* to help her replace comparison with truth.

What the Bible Says: Boundaries Are Love, Not Control

Proverbs 22:6 says:

"Start children off on how they should go; even when they are old, they will not turn from it."

Think of boundaries like guardrails on a winding mountain road. They're there to keep her safe and on the path God wants her to take—not to trap or control her.

Facing Today's Challenges: Boundaries in a Digital World

When you see your daughter struggling with social media, self-image, or peer pressure, take a deep breath before reacting. Instead of shutting her down, ask gentle questions that open the door to honest conversation. Read Scripture together that reminds her she is beautifully made just as she is.

Real Talk: Making Boundaries Together

Mike and Teresa always set a 9:30 p.m. curfew for their daughter Skye. But instead of just enforcing it, they sat down and asked:

"What do you think is a fair curfew, and why?"

Skye suggested 11:00 p.m., explaining most activities wind down then. They compromised at 10:30 p.m. and agreed she'd check in if plans changed. Suddenly, rules didn't feel like punishment—they felt like respect.

Grace Is at the Heart of Discipline

Hebrews 12:11 says:

"No discipline seems pleasant at the time but painful. Later on, however, it produces a harvest of righteousness and peace for those trained by it."

Discipline isn't about making her miserable. It's about shaping her character and building peace.

A Story of Correction with Love

Faith, 16, told her parents she was going to the mall, but she actually went to a boy's house instead. When her dad found out, he didn't yell or shame her. He said:

"I'm more worried about why you had to lie."

They talked, prayed, and read Ephesians 4:25:

"Therefore, you must put off falsehood and speak truthfully..."

Faith apologized and rebuilt trust—not because she was afraid, but because she knew she was loved.

Here's what you can do: Stay calm. Ask "why," not just "what." Discipline with love through prayer, conversation, and forgiveness.

Helping Her Set Her Limits

When Ayana got invited to a wild after-prom party, her mom didn't say "No." Instead, she asked:

"What choice will make you proud ten years from now?"

That question helped Ayana see she was made to lead, not just fit in. She said no and instead hosted a small praise night with friends.

Grace Gives Strength to Say No

Titus 2:11-12 says:

"For the grace of God has appeared... It teaches us to say 'No' to ungodliness and worldly passions and to live self-controlled, upright and godly lives."

What you can do: Encourage your daughter to pray daily for grace and courage to say "No." Remind her that boundaries aren't walls but bridges to better choices.

Wrap-Up: Boundaries That Point Back to Jesus

Your daughter will one day make choices when you're not watching. When she understands *why* boundaries exist, she'll respect them—not because she's afraid, but because she knows they come from love. This understanding can give you a sense of accomplishment, knowing that your efforts in setting and maintaining boundaries are practical and successful.

Let your home be where boundaries are explained patiently, discipline is discipleship, and mistakes are met with mercy.

Challenge for Parents: Think About Your Boundaries

- Are your rules clear, or are they just assumed?
- Do you explain *why* those boundaries matter?
- Do you invite your daughter to help set boundaries?
- Does your discipline bring her closer to Christ or focus on punishment?

A Prayer for You

God, give me wisdom to guide my daughter with love and courage. Help me set boundaries that build her character and discipline that reflects Your heart. When I feel overwhelmed, remind me that You love her even more than I do and work on her even when I can't see it. Amen.

Chapter 10:
Life Skills Every Teen Girl Needs
(That School Might Not Teach)

No matter where your daughter's going next— college, a job, or something unexpected—she'll need more than good grades. She'll need life skills to navigate the messy, beautiful, and confusing world.

Here's the hard truth: most schools won't teach her these.

You're Not Alone if You're Wondering...
"What if I don't know how to teach her these things? What if I mess it all up?"

I get it. Many parents feel this way, and it's perfectly understandable. What matters is that you show up—with love, patience, and faith.

What the Bible Teaches Us: Real Parents, Real Lessons
The Bible is filled with stories of parents who faced tough choices.

Jochebed: The Mom Who Trusted God
Moses' mom faced a terrifying choice—Pharaoh wanted to kill all Hebrew baby boys. She protected Moses, then made a scary but faithful decision to place him in a basket, trusting God to keep him safe.

Sometimes, parenting means letting go of faith. We teach, prepare, and trust God with what we can't control.

Eli: The Dad Who Didn't Step Up

Eli was a priest who failed to correct his sons' bad choices. His story reminds us that ignoring problems doesn't help—kids need boundaries, correction, and love, even when it's hard.

Stories from Today: What Works and What Doesn't

Sarah and Mike: Talking Money

Sarah, a single mom, taught her daughter budgeting after they struggled with debt. Instead of lecturing, they sat down weekly to plan together. Now, her daughter manages money with confidence and prays about financial choices.

Money is more than math—it's about honouring God with what He's given us. Open talks build trust.

John's Silence: What Happens When We Don't Talk

John thought ignoring his daughter's anxiety was the best way. Instead, she felt alone and started making poor choices. This shows us how important emotional health is—and that parents must listen, even when it's tough.

How Real Parents Instill Life Skills—Whether Your Daughter Is Lazy, Willing, or Just... Meh

Start early if you can. But if it feels "late"? Start anyway.

God doesn't need perfect timing. He works with mustard seeds.

Real Parents, Real Tensions

Maybe you're the mom who feels the clock ticking.

You *want* to pass everything on—how to cook, budget, and hold her head high when life hits low. But she doesn't always want to hear it. And you wonder if she's even listening.

Maybe you're the dad who wants her **ready**.

Not perfect. Just prepared—for life, for work, for the world. You're okay if she learns from YouTube, a coach, or a part-time job. You don't want her blindsided by the stuff no one teaches.

And then there's your daughter.

Is she:

- **Lazy?** Distracted. Unmotivated. Easily overwhelmed.
- **Willing?** Curious. Open. Not perfect, but ready to try.
- **Neutral?** Not pushing back, not leaning in. Just... cruising.

Each girl needs something different. And each parent brings something sacred.

1. Ruth & Naomi: The Willing Daughter Who Learned by Walking Together

Life Skill: Adaptability, wise decisions, spiritual grounding

Naomi didn't pull a scroll and say, *"Here are the top 10 ways to thrive in Bethlehem."*

She let Ruth *watch her life*—grieving, moving, working, trusting.

Ruth followed. Not because Naomi lectured—but because she lived it.

What Parents Can Do:
- Invite your daughter into your real life: grocery lists, career decisions, even mistakes.

- Let her see how you lean on God—not just preach it.

"When my daughter said, 'I want to be independent like you,' I stopped doing everything for her. We meal plan now. She shops. She budgets. And I... watch her grow."
— **Sandra, mom of 17-year-old Janae**

2. Lauren & the Egg Budget: The Lazy Teen Who Learned by Struggle

Life Skill: Budgeting, responsibility, and waiting well
Lauren didn't care.

She burned toast. She overdrafted her account. Her parents, Marcus and Tasha, had finally stopped nagging.

So they handed her **$30** and said:

"You're in charge of breakfast this week."

She blew the budget in two days and had to eat eggs the rest of the week.

She was furious.

"You set me up to fail."

They listened. Debriefed. It didn't rescue her.

Three months later, she was **meal-prepping** and **price-matching** better than her mom.

"I hated them for it. Now I'm the only one of my friends who doesn't panic when rent's due." – Lauren, 19

3. Abigail: The Neutral Daughter Who Rose in Crisis

Life Skill: Emotional regulation, clear thinking, relational wisdom
Abigail didn't raise her hand. She wasn't the star pupil.

But when everything was falling apart, **she acted with poise and strategy**.

She *stepped up*—not because she was constantly coached, but because **seeds were planted**.

Her parents may have quietly modelled grace, restraint, and wisdom. She absorbed it.

Not every lesson takes root immediately. But it's still being planted.

4. Madison & the Flat Tire: A Neutral Daughter Finds Her Power

Life Skill: Problem-solving and independence
Madison wasn't lazy—but she wasn't interested.

Her dad, James, wanted her to feel capable, not coddled.

So he **faked a flat tyre**.

"You're *gonna change it today.*"

She groaned. She rolled her eyes. Muttered.

But she did it. Slowly. Complaining. But learning.

After, he said:

"If it happens at night, you won't freeze up. You're stronger than you think."

She now teaches the same skill to her college friends.

> *"She didn't say thank you. But I saw the shift—confidence in her stride."* — **James, dad of 18-year-old Madison.**

5. Mary: The Girl with God's Assignment and Her Parents' Preparation

Life Skill: Trust, spiritual maturity, emotional stability

Mary didn't *become* brave the moment Gabriel appeared.

She'd been shaped by parents who *taught her to trust God in the quiet years.*

When the angel came, she was ready to say, *"Let it be to me according to Your word."*

That doesn't come from nowhere.

What Parents Can Do:
- Talk to God in front of her.
- Let her see you obey when it's inconvenient.
- Let faith be *honest*, not just *routine*.

"Your job isn't to make her fearless. It's to help her know where to run when fear comes."

6. Maria & Ellie: The Overachiever Mom and Her Stressed-Out Daughter

Life Skill: Time management and stress recovery
Maria wanted to pass on *everything*:

Planners. Systems. Hacks. Color-coded tabs.

But Ellie?

I didn't care. Overwhelmed. Shut down.

Maria finally stopped pushing.

She asked, *"What do you want to be good at?"*

Ellie said, *"I don't want to feel this stressed."*

So they started **5-minute calming routines** after school.

That turned into **self-scheduling**.

One day? Ellie asked for a planner.

Her choice. Her rhythm. Her growth.
"I cried in the bathroom. I wanted to force growth. But God whispered—'Let her grow. Not just go.'"

Word to Parents

Whether she's lazy, willing, or neutral...

- **Let her experience the need.** Don't just explain it.
- **Trust the slow work of God.**
- **Trade control for connection.**
- **Teach, but also watch. Let her become.**

What Dads Bring:
- Focus and function: *"Here's what she needs before she leaves."*
- Realism: *"If we can't teach it, we'll pay for someone who can."*

What Moms Bring:
- Deep emotion: *"I want her to have what I never did."*
- Heart-level legacy: *"I want her to be a better me."*

But both must learn to **release**, not just *instil*.

What Makes Life Skills Stick:
1. **Experience > Explanation**
2. **Mistakes = Mentors**
3. **Patience Must Be Modeled**
4. **Prayer Isn't Plan B—it's the foundation**
5. **Faith Doesn't Replace Skills. It Empowers Them.**

You're not just preparing her for adulthood.

You're shaping a woman who will face the world with grace, grit, and God.

And even if she forgets the recipe or the budgeting app—

She'll remember the look in your eyes when she finally got it right.

She'll remember the warmth of your "I'm proud of you."

She'll remember the faith that carried you—and is now holding her.

What Parents Want (But Don't Always Find)

From parents conversation meeting, parents evenings, counselling and listening to parents, here's what they say they need:

- Simple, straightforward advice on teaching life skills like budgeting, cooking, and managing stress.
- Faith that feels real, not preachy.
- Honest talk about struggles and doubts.
- Support for moms and dads—because dads want to help, too!
- Ways to connect so teens feel more open.

This book is here to fill that gap. It's for you, your family, your faith journey.

How to Start Teaching Life Skills—The Easy Way

1. **Pray and Listen**

    Pray for your daughter. Listen when she talks.

2. **Find Out What She Needs Most**

    Does she struggle with money? Time? Stress? Start there.

3. **Use Everyday Moments**

    Car rides, meals, and even fights can become lessons.

4. **Show Your Faith**

    Be honest about your struggles and how God helps you.

5. **Let Her Make Mistakes (Safely)**

    Mistakes aren't failures—they're lessons.

6. **Build Community**

   Encourage friendships, mentorship, and involvement in the church. No one parents alone.

Life Skills She Needs to Know
- Budgeting and money management
- Problem-solving and decision-making
- Managing time and priorities
- Basic cooking and self-care
- Handling stress and emotions
- Trusting God daily

A Word to You

Parenting a teen girl isn't easy. Some days, you'll wonder if you're making a difference. But like Sarah from the Bible—who laughed, doubted, yet kept faith—keep believing.

Like Jochebed, trust God when you have to let go.

You don't have to be perfect. Just keep showing up, praying, and loving.

Because you're raising more than a daughter—you're raising a woman who will change the world.

Chapter 11:
Looking Ahead
College, Careers, and What Comes Next

The future is exciting, but at the same time, it is also very scary. Your role is evolving as your daughter stands on the threshold of adulthood. You're no longer the one with all the answers; instead, you become her coach, cheerleader, and prayer partner. This chapter is designed to equip *you*—the loving parent—to help her step confidently into what lies ahead.

Because here's the truth: Your daughter's future isn't just about getting a job or a degree. It's about *living out God's unique calling* on her life, even if it looks very different from what anyone expected.

Helping Her Navigate Career and Education Choices

Let's be real. Choosing a career path can feel like navigating a noisy, crowded crossroads. There's pressure everywhere—social media telling her what's "cool," well-meaning family pushing "safe" options, and teachers handing out advice that might not fit her. It's easy to get lost or doubt herself.

Your daughter needs more than career advice—she needs a foundation rooted in faith and self-discovery.

Look at Joanne. His parents supported her interest in engineering—not because it was "safe," but because Joanne's passion was solving real-world problems. She wanted to build clean water systems for communities in need. For Joannes, career and calling were inseparable.

When a job aligns with God's purpose, your daughter won't just work—she'll *thrive*.

Mia's Story: Finding Courage to Follow Her Path

Mia was 17 — a whirlwind of creativity, always sketching, dreaming, and thinking outside the box. While most of her friends were chasing careers in law or medicine, Mia lit up when she talked about graphic design.

But every time she shared her passion, the questions came:

"Is that even a real job?"

"Don't you want something more secure?"

"You're so smart — you could do more."

Little by little, those doubts started to sink in. She began to question if her dream really mattered.

Then one evening at dinner, something shifted — and everything began to change.

Her dad asked, "If money wasn't a thing, what would you want to do daily?"

Mia paused for a second, then quietly said, "I want to create art that inspires people—designs that reflect God's truth and beauty to showcase and make God visible."

Her mom looked at her gently and asked, "And how does that make you feel?"

Mia smiled. "Alive," she said. "Like it's not just a job… it's worship."

Her dad nodded and began sharing stories of Christian artists who were using their creativity to make a real impact. "You don't have to choose between your faith and your career," he told her. "They're meant to go hand in hand."

For the first time, Mia felt *permission*—not just to dream, but to plan.

How You Can Help Your Daughter Find God's Purpose in Her Career

Do:
- Ask heart-focused questions: "What breaks your heart?" "What problems do you want to solve?"
- Help her discover her God-given gifts—not just her grades.
- Encourage daily prayer for wisdom and clarity.
- Share inspiring stories of faith-led careers.
- Support internships, volunteering, or shadowing in her areas of interest.

Don't:
- Pressure her into "safe" careers out of fear.
- Shame her for unconventional dreams.
- Compare her to others—her path is *unique*.
- Ignore God in career conversations—this is a Kingdom decision.

Rooting Career Choices in Grace and Prayer

Remind her that clarity grows with grace.

> *"God gives grace to the humble." — **James 4:6***

Encourage her to pray:

"God, show me who You made me to be. Open the right doors. Close the wrong ones. Give me grace to walk confidently in Your plan, even if it looks different than I imagined."

When she sees her career as a sacred calling, worldly success becomes secondary to purpose.

Preparing for the College Transition

College is more than moving away—a massive spiritual and emotional shift. Excitement mixes with nerves, and your daughter might worry about staying true to her faith amid new freedoms and pressures.

Mike and Rachel's Pre-College Moment

Mike noticed his daughter Rachel growing quiet as the move-in day neared. Sitting with her, he gently asked, "What's on your mind?"

Rachel admitted, "What if I lose myself there? What if I can't handle it?"

Mike replied, "College won't change who you are but will show who you're becoming. Do you know who that is?"

They talked honestly about faith, loneliness, and temptation. Mike reminded her that God's grace never runs out—whether at home or on campus at 2 a.m. He encouraged Rachel to find a Christian community quickly, rather than waiting for friends to come to her.

Rachel left feeling equipped—not because she had every answer, but because she *knew* she wasn't alone.

How You Can Help Your Daughter Prepare Spiritually and Emotionally for College

Do:
- Have honest talks about identity, temptation, and loneliness.
- Help her connect with local churches, ministries, or campus groups.
- Teach wise decision-making *before* pressure hits.
- Remind her God's love is unconditional—even when she stumbles.
- Pray *with* and *for* her regularly.

Don't:
- Assume church attendance equals spiritual strength.
- Focus only on academics; emotional and spiritual readiness matter most.
- Avoid tough topics like alcohol, sex, or anxiety.
- Use guilt instead of grace.

Encouraging Independence While Staying Connected

Your daughter is becoming an adult. She needs room to grow—and a lifeline back to you. Maintain open communication through regular calls, texts, and visits even when you don't have positive response. Offer guidance, but honour her autonomy.

Trusting God with Her Future

Remember: her future is *in God's hands*. Your job is to love, support, pray, and share wisdom.

Through your steady love and wise encouragement, you're helping your daughter step into a future rooted in faith, purpose, and grace.

Chapter 12:
Love, Friendships, and Everything in Between

As your daughter moves into young adulthood, the people she surrounds herself with—friends from school, family, neighbours and others—begin to shape her world in deep and meaningful ways. These relationships become the heartbeat of her daily life, influencing how she feels, what she believes, and how she sees herself. This season will be filled with bright, joyful moments, messy challenges, and meaningful opportunities for you—as a parent—to walk alongside her with patience, empathy, and real, honest love. It's in these everyday moments that your steady support and kindness can truly change the course of her journey.

Friendships: From Fake Friends to Faithful Sisters
Teen years often feel like a whirlwind of friendships—some uplifting, others painful. But friendships aren't just about popularity or fitting in; they are about purpose and spiritual growth.

A Tale of Two Prayers: Kate & Victoria
Kate, a lively sophomore, once made what she called a "Friend Wishlist" and prayed as if she were placing an Amazon order. Weeks later, at church camp, she met Amara, Zoe, and Faith—girls who loved Jesus, shared her quirky sense of humour, and kept drama far

away. Their bond blossomed over late-night Chick-fil-A devotions and Bible TikToks, creating a friendship grounded in faith and fun.

Victoria's story was more harrowing. She prayed just as fervently but faced teasing from classmates who mocked her for saying "God bless you" or carrying a Bible. Hurt and frustrated, Victoria cried, "God, this isn't fair!" But she didn't stop praying. Instead, she prayed for the very girls who hurt her—Chloe and Hannah. "Lord, they irritate me," she admitted, "but I won't stop praying for them until You change their hearts."

Months later, when Victoria faced her struggles, she responded with love, not bitterness. Chloe eventually asked, "Why didn't you give up on us?" That question became the doorway for Victoria to share her faith. Today, Chloe and Hannah are part of her Bible study group, having confessed their harshness was rooted in pain at home, not hatred of God. Victoria's story reminds us of Job 42:10, "The Lord restored Job's fortunes when he prayed for his friends."

Biblical Wisdom for Friendships: Choosing Companions for the Journey

Proverbs 13:20 teaches, "Walk with the wise and become wise, for a companion of fools suffers harm." Friendships are not just social—they are spiritual. The people your daughter surrounds herself with will either sharpen her faith or dull her Spirit.

Help her understand that we are united in the Body of Christ as believers. Every friend carries a piece of God's wisdom and grace; her spiritual growth will often happen through these relationships. When she chooses friends who reflect God's character, she is not merely being safe but spiritually nurtured.

The Road and the Tires: A Visual on Friendship

Imagine life as a long journey with smooth highways and rocky detours. Friendships are like the tyres that keep the car moving forward.

- Healthy, Christ-centered friendships are strong, steady tyres that carry her through every bump.
- Toxic friendships—those filled with gossip, lies, manipulation, or peer pressure—are like nails on the road that cause flat tyres and stall her journey.

Consider these spiritual "flat tyres":
- Gossip is a slow leak.
- Lies are sharp punctures.
- Manipulation is a hidden gash.
- Peer pressure is losing control of the steering wheel.

These aren't just social challenges—they damage her Spirit.

Teaching Her to Spot the Warning Signs

Help your daughter develop spiritual discernment by asking:
- "Do you feel stronger in your faith after being with them?"
- "Can you be your true self in Christ around these friends?"
- "Do they encourage your convictions or wear them down?"

Remind her that setting boundaries when relationships pull her away from God's calling is not just okay—it's godly.

Nurturing Friendships That Sharpen Faith

Encourage her to seek friends who:

- Speak the truth with kindness, not just flattery
- Pray with her, not just party with her

- Celebrate her calling, not compete with it
- Hold her accountable, not hold her hostage

The deepest friendships are quiet but powerful—rooted in shared values and eternal purpose. Show her how you choose wise friends and walk with grace and truth.

Dating: Flirting with the World or Falling into God's Plan?

Today's dating can feel like navigating a minefield wearing glamorous but risky flip—flops. Between filtered social media stories and peer pressure whispering, "Just go with it," many teens wonder, "Is it even possible to date God's way anymore?"

The answer is yes—but it takes intention, wisdom, and Jesus at the centre.

Hannah & Adam: Dating with Purpose and Prayer

When Hannah met Adam, they didn't start with flirting or DMs. Instead, they shared a hunger for a relationship that glorified God, not just gratified feelings. They made a pact: "If we date, it will be on purpose and with purpose."

Their first challenge was a 14-day social media fast—no scrolling, Snapping, or TikTok. They replaced noise with God's Word, praying daily, sharing God's teaching, and holding each other accountable.

Their Spiritual Goals:

1. **Memorizing Scripture Weekly:** They quizzed each other every Sunday and posted verses as reminders.

2. **Praying for Their School:** Daily prayer, voice notes, lifted teachers and classmates.

3. **Sharing Testimonies:** At a youth event, Hannah shared her journey from fear of rejection to boldness for Christ; Adam shared his victory over temptation through God's strength.

Hannah's Story: From Fear of Rejection to Boldness for Christ

Hannah often smiled on cue but felt invisible inside. She sought acceptance by altering her appearance and behaviour. One night, scrolling through perfect online lives, she broke down, praying honestly for the first time in a long while: "God, if You still want the real me... I'm here."

She deleted old pictures, unfollowed toxic influencers, and began sharing her real struggles and God's truth. Her courage helped other girls find freedom, proving that surrendering —not strength—brings true healing.

Adam's Struggle

Adam bravely shared his struggle with pornography—a hidden battle many face but few talk about. A youth camp retreat became his turning point. He sought help, set firm boundaries, and leaned on God's strength daily.

His vulnerability opened doors for healing—not just for himself but for others, like Nick, a friend who approached him for support.

Handling Temptation Together

One quiet night after worship, hands touched, hearts raced, and temptation loomed. Hannah said, "We should stop." Adam agreed.

They didn't pretend it wasn't real. Instead, they confided in a trusted mentor and prayed for strength. Their honesty built a foundation of holiness—beyond actions into thoughts.

Guiding Your Daughter to Date God's Way

Teach her that:

- Dating isn't about finding a Savior but walking with someone who knows the Savior.
- Physical purity starts with mental purity.
- God cares about how she dates, not just who she dates.
- Real love sets boundaries, not just follows feelings.
- Confessing struggles early is a sign of strength, not weakness.

Ask:

- "Do you pray together?"
- "Are you growing closer to God through this relationship or despite it?"
- "What's the spiritual plan, not just the emotional pull?"

Sarah & Josh: From Hype to Hurt to Healing

Sarah fell for Josh, who was charming but not a believer in love. She hoped he'd change her, but instead, she changed. Boundaries were crossed, worship felt empty, and God seemed distant. After confessing to her parents and pastor, she began healing. Like a deflated tyre, her Spirit was restored through repentance, accountability, and grace.

Sarah learned that godly relationships prepare us for marriage through intentional courtship (1 Thessalonians 4:3–7).

Real Lessons from Real Girls

This chapter isn't just a list of tips—it's a lifeline for parents and daughters as they navigate today's messy, beautiful, and sometimes complicated world of love and friendship. Rooted in timeless biblical truth and made real through everyday stories, this will be helping you walk with your daughter as she learns to make choices that honour God, protect her heart, and lead her toward a future full of hope, meaning, and purpose.

Chapter 13:
Motherhood That Leaves a Legacy:
12 Real-Life Lessons from the Frontlines

Mother's Teaching # 1: A Heart-to-Heart Conversation About Your Period
(A Tender Talk Between a Mom and Her Daughter)

Mom: *[Sitting down on the couch beside her daughter, giving her a soft smile]*

"Hey, sweetheart, can we chat for a minute? I've been meaning to talk to you about something important. How are you feeling today?"

Daughter: *[Shrugs a little, a bit unsure]*

"I'm good, I guess... but I'm kinda tired. Why?"

Mom: *[Rubbing her daughter's back very gently]*

"Well, I wanted to talk to you about something that's coming up soon, something normal, but I want you to feel prepared. It's about your period. I know you've heard some things from your friends or even at school, and I want to make sure you know exactly what's going on when it happens. Does that sound okay?"

Daughter: *[glancing up, softly]* "Um... when does it happen? How will I know?"

Mom: [sits beside her] "Well, you might notice a few signs first—like your breasts growing, or new hairs under your arms or down below. Sometimes there's a whitish discharge a while before the period—like a little heads-up from your body."

Daughter: [fiddling with her fingers] "Okay... but what about the bleeding—how will I notice?"

Mom: "It usually starts with a little spotting—maybe brown, then brighter red. You might feel some cramps or a bit of discomfort but it's usually light at first. It can last a few days up to a week."

Daughter: [brows furrowing a bit] "That sounds... kinda scary?"

Mom: [smiling gently] "It might feel strange at first, but it's perfectly normal. Lots of girls start feeling this way—you're growing up, and your body is just doing what it's supposed to. Everyone goes through it."

Daughter: [nodding slowly] "So... what do I do when it starts?"

Mom: "You can use a pad—just stick it in your underwear and change it every few hours. If you're ever not sure, just ask me or another grown-up. You'll learn as you go."

Daughter: [smiles a little] "Okay. Will I need things at school?"

Mom: "Just in case, I'll pack pads in your bag. Maybe even a spare pair of knickers—so you're ready, wherever you are."

Mom: [softly] "If you ever feel weird or have questions—about your body, your feelings—anything—you can come to me. No question is silly, and you're never alone in this very one."

Mom: *[Pauses for a moment, making sure her tone is gentle and reassuring]*

"Great question, sweetie. You might notice that you start feeling a little crampy or tired before the bleeding happens. At first, it might be light, just a little spotting. But then, your period will come a few times each month, and you'll get a better sense of how your body works. You might get cramps or feel bloated. That's all normal."

Daughter: *[Looking a little worried]*

"Will it hurt? How do I deal with it if it does?"

Mom: *[Taking her daughter's hand gently]*

"It might hurt a bit. It's like your tummy or your lower back tightening up. Some girls have it very badly, while others have a little. But don't worry, there are things you can do to make it better. You can use a **heating pad** on your abdomen or take medication, such as ibuprofen, to help alleviate the pain. And if you're feeling tired, it's okay to rest. You can take it easy, by watching a movie, or just nap."

Daughter: *[Nods slowly, still a little very unsure but feeling comforted]*

"Okay... that doesn't sound too bad, I guess. But what if I forget to change my pad or tampon? I don't want to mess up or get it all over my clothes."

Mom: *[Laughing softly, brushing a piece of hair behind her daughter's ear]*

"Sweetie, it's okay if you forget sometimes. You're still learning, and I'm here to help you figure it out. When you start your period, you'll use something called a **pad** or a **tampon** to catch the blood. Pads are simple; you wear them inside your underwear, and they absorb everything. You should change them every 4-6 hours, but you'll get a feel for it over time. Just make sure you always have a backup in your bag or your room, and if you feel like you might leak, you can always check and change it."

Daughter: "Okay, so pads are easy to use. What if I use a tampon instead?"

Mom: *[Nodding thoughtfully]*

"Tampons are a little different, but I know some girls prefer them because they're less noticeable. You insert them inside your body, but you should change them every 4-6 hours as well. We'll talk more about tampons when you're ready, but for now, let's stick with pads. And remember—always wash your hands before and after you change them."

Daughter: "Got it. Change it often, and wash my hands. But... what about if it's super heavy or light?"

"Good observation. At first, your period might be lighter, and you might not need to change your pad as often. But as your body gets used to it, sometimes the flow will get heavier, and you'll need to change your pad more often. It's all part of the adjustment, so don't worry if it's different each time. Heavy or light, we'll figure out what works for you together. Just rememember, whatever you experience, it's all a really normal and part of growing up."

Daughter: *[Thinking for a second, then speaking up]*

"Okay, so what do I do if it's like... hurting too much? I've heard my friends talk about cramps. How do I deal with those?"

Mom: *[Nods understandingly]*

"Cramps can be a pain, I know. But there's a lot you can do. First of all, some **rest** helps a lot. If you're feeling tired or sore, relax. A warm **heating pad** on your belly or lower back works wonders for cramps. I also have some medicine like ibuprofen that we can use to ease the pain. You can always ask me if you need anything."

Daughter: "Okay, I'll try the heating pad. That sounds like it would help. And what about food? Is there anything I should eat or avoid?"

Mom: *[Thinking carefully, then smiling]*

During your period, you might notice some changes in your mood. It's normal to feel a bit more emotional or very irritable. Just remember, it's okay to feel this way, and it's not your fault. If you ever feel overwhelmed, just let me know, and we can talk about it. "Well, you'll want to drink lots of **water**—that's always a good idea. Eating **fruits** and **vegetables** will help, too, because they keep you hydrated and healthy. **Iron-rich foods** like spinach or lean meats can help your body replace the iron it loses during your period. Try to stay away from too many **sugary snacks** or **salty foods** because they can make you feel bloated or grumpy. If you want a snack, try some nuts or fruit instead."

"You're doing very great, sweetheart. You're learning about something new and important, and really I'm so proud of you. Remember, you're strong and capable, and you can handle this."

"Okay, I can do that. And what about, like, my hair and skin? I've noticed that I'm breaking out a little more lately."

Mom: *[Chuckling softly]*

"Ah, yes, the joys of growing up! Your skin and hair will change during your period. It's normal to get a little oilier, especially on your face and scalp. Just keep washing your face and using gentle shampoo for your hair. You might want to wash your hair a little more often during your period to keep it fresh. It's all part of your body adjusting."

Daughter: "I guess that's okay. But I have to remember to keep my room clean, too, right?"

Mom: *[Laughing lightly]*

"Yes, sweetie. Keeping your room neat as it helps you feel very organized and in control. And when you're done with used pads or tampons, make sure to dispose of them properly. Wrap them up in toilet paper or a bag and throw them in the trash—don't flush them down the toilet. Trust me, the plumbing will thank you!"

Daughter: *[Smiling now, feeling more relaxed]*

"I think I can handle all that very well. But what about Dad? Is he supposed to do anything?"

Mom: *[Nods lovingly]*

"Your dad can help too, sweetie. He might not fully understand what it feels like to have a period, but he'll still be there to support you. He can make sure you have what you need, like pads or pain relief, and he can give you a little extra care when you're feeling uncomfortable. And if you ever need anything, you know he will be there to listen. Dads need to show love and support during this time, just like I am."

Daughter: *[Smiling softly, feeling reassured]*

"Thanks, Mom. I feel a lot better about all of these. I'm not so scared anymore."

Mom: *[Hugging her daughter tightly]*

"You're welcome, sweet girl. You're growing up very beautifully, and I'm so proud of you. And remember, this is one of the steps in the amazing journey God has for you. You're never alone in this—I'm always here, and your dad is too. You're loved, always."

Daughter: *[Hugging her back, feeling loved and secure]*

"I love you too, Mom. Thanks for talking to me about all of this."

Mother's Teaching # 2: A Heart-to-Heart About Caring for Our Bodies

A warm, honest family moment

Mom: *[Sitting on the couch with a thoughtful look, patting the cushions]*

"Come sit, you two. I've been thinking a lot lately, and I want to have a little heart-to-heart. As you both grow older, it's really important we talk about how we take care of ourselves—not just our appearance, but our bodies, our health, and how all of that ties into honouring God."

Daughter: *[Curious but cautious]*

"Okay… are we talking, like, hygiene? Or something deeper?"

Mom: *[Smiling gently]*

"Both. Hygiene is part of it, but it's also about respect—respecting the body God gave you, understanding the changes you're going through, and taking care of yourself in a way that reflects who you are inside. And yes, Adam, you're part of this conversation too."

Son 1 (Adam): *[A bit hesitant, but open]*

"Wait, even stuff about girls? Like bras and stuff?"

Mom: *[Warmly]*

"Yes, Adam. It might feel awkward, but understanding what your sister or female friends experience will help you become a kinder, more thoughtful man. And Abigail, the same goes for you—knowing what boys go through will help you show empathy and support."

Son 2: *[Trying to be cool, but clearly intrigued]*

"Alright, let's go. What do we need to know?"

1. Bras, Underwear, and Dressing with Confidence and Respect

Mom: *[Turning to her daughter]*

"Abigail, as your body changes, it's important to find undergarments that make you feel comfortable and very confident. A well-fitted bra isn't just about support—it's about how you carry yourself through the day. And Adam, this is something that most girls think about every single day."

Abigail: *[Quietly]*

"I think I've outgrown mine, but I didn't want to say anything."

Mom: *[Smiling reassuringly]*

"That's perfectly normal, sweetheart. We'll go together and get you fitted. There's no rush, and no shame. And remember—what we wear under our clothes matters too. Clean, comfortable underwear in breathable fabrics helps you feel fresh and confident."

Adam: *[Trying to understand]*

"So... it's about support and feeling comfortable in your body?"

Mom: *[Nods]*

"Exactly. It helps girls not feel self-conscious. And when you understand that, Adam, you're less likely to make someone feel embarrassed. It's all part of being respectful."

2. Clean Towels, Sheets & Why It Matters
Mom:

"Let's talk about something simple but often overlooked—laundry. Towels and bedding collect everything from sweat to skin cells, and if we don't clean them regularly, they become a breeding ground for bacteria."

Adam: *[Groans]*

"But it's just a towel, Mom."

Mom: *[Laughing softly]*

"Yes, but that towel touches your skin every day. Once a week, okay? Same with your pillowcases—they're pressed against your face all night!"

Abigail: *[Nods]*

"I guess I should be better about that. My pillow gets oily."

3. Smelling Good—Not Overwhelming
Mom: *[With a playful but very serious tone]*

"Alright, let's talk body odor. It's real. It's natural. And it's avoidable. Daily showers are essential, especially as your bodies start changing more. And deodorant is your friend. For both of you."

Adam:

"No one wants to be the stinky one."

Son 2:

"I've been using deodorant more. And I even sprayed cologne last week."

Mom: *[Chuckles]*

"Just don't bathe in it, okay? A little is nice, but too much can make people uncomfortable. Smelling fresh is a way of showing respect—not just to yourself, but to everyone around you."

4. Teeth, Skin, and Self-Care
Mom:

"Brushing your teeth twice a day is great. But flossing? That's what keeps your gums healthy. It's the extra step that saves you pain in the long run."

Abigail:

"Flossing takes forever."

Mom:

"I know. But you're investing in your smile—your future self will thank you. Same with skincare. Drink water. Moisturize. And wash your face at night."

Adam:

"Okay, okay, I'll do it. I like having good skin anyway."

5. Hair, Feet, and the Little Things That Matter
Mom:

"Haircare is about cleanliness, not just style. And feet—don't forget them! Wash them every day. If they smell, deal with it. There's nothing wrong with needing foot powder or clean socks."

Son 2: *[Laughing very loudly]*

"Alright, alright—I don't want anyone passing out next to me!"

6. Modesty & Respecting Ourselves and Others
Mom: *[Looking both kids in the eye]*

"I want you both to understand modesty—not as something strict or old-fashioned, but as a way of honouring your body. You don't need to show everything to feel confident. True confidence is quiet. It's in how you speak, how you carry yourself, and how you treat others."

Abigail: *[Thoughtful]*

"So modesty isn't about being ashamed. It's about being secure?"

Mom: *[Gently, with a warm smile]*

" Exactly. You're not hiding who you are, you're protecting what's sacred.

Mom: *[Beaming]*

"That's right. Taking care of yourself isn't just physical—it's spiritual. It says, 'I honour the body God gave me.' And when you do that, you naturally treat others with that same honour."

Abigail: *[Leans in, hugs her mom]*

"Thanks for talking to us like this, Mom. I feel like I understand things better now."

Son 2: *[Grinning]*

"Alright, I'm off to wash my feet. And floss. And maybe moisturize. I'm all in!"

Mother's Teaching # 3: A Heart-to-Heart Discussion About Finance and Stewardship

Mom: [Sitting down at the kitchen table, looking very serious yet inviting]

"Alright, guys, today we're going to have an important talk about money—how to manage it, save it, and use it in a way that honours God. This is something everyone needs to learn, no matter how old you are. I want you both to understand that how we handle money is part of our Christian walk and how we steward the resources God gives us."

Son 1: [Leaning back in his chair, looking very intrigued]

"Okay, Mom. We're talking about money, but what do you mean by 'honouring God with it'? Is it about saving or what?"

Mom: [Nodding]

"Yes, saving is very important, but it's about so much more than just saving. It's about understanding that money isn't ours to begin with. It's all a gift from God. Everything we have comes from Him, and He's entrusted us with these resources to be good stewards of them. So, I want to teach you both how to be wise with money in a way that glorifies God."

Daughter: [Sitting up, looking very curious]

"I don't know much about money. I have a piggy bank, but I don't think that's what you mean."

Mom: [Laughing softly, shaking her head]

"A piggy bank is a good start, but we're going to talk about budgeting, saving, and giving. These are the principles that will help you manage money when you start earning it as an adult. And it's never too early to learn. The earlier you understand these things, the better off you'll be."

1. Understanding Money: It's a Tool, Not the Goal

Mom: [Leaning forward, speaking very gently but firmly]

"First, let's talk about the purpose of money. Money is a tool. It's not the goal. The Bible tells us in Matthew 6:24 that 'No one can serve two masters. Either you will hate the one and love the other, or you will be devoted to the one and despise the other.' So, money should never become the thing you chase after or love above all else."

Son 2: [Looking confused]

"So, you're saying we shouldn't care about money?"

Mom:

"Not exactly. Caring about money means understanding its purpose and using it very wisely. But loving money is different. When money becomes your main focus, it can pull you away from God and the things that matter—your faith, your family, and serving others. We are called to be good stewards of what God gives us. Stewardship is about managing your money in a way that honours Him."

Daughter: [Nodding very slowly]

"That makes sense. So, money isn't bad, but loving it is what is wrong."

The Importance of Saving, Budgeting, and Tithing Mom: [Turning to both kids, smiling and gently folding her hands on her lap]: "Alright, you two—now let's get into the real-life stuff: saving, budgeting, and yes, tithing. This is where faith meets everyday life. The Bible talks a lot about being wise stewards of what we have, and that means we don't just spend as we feel—we plan.

Even if you're only getting a little pocket money, or someone gives you a gift, or you earn something from helping out somewhere—it's so important to start thinking about *how* you use it.

It's not about having a lot; it's about learning to be faithful with the little you have now. That's what builds discipline, and trust with God. You set something aside to save, something for your needs, and something—*always something*—to give back to God. That's tithing. Not because He needs our money, but because it reminds us that everything we have comes from Him in the first place."

Son 1: [Looking serious now]

"I get that. But how do we even start saving? I mean, what should I do with the money that I get?"

Mom:

"Great question. Saving starts with understanding that not all of the money you receive is for spending. A good rule of thumb is to put aside at least 10% of what you get into savings. The Bible speaks about tithing, and giving a portion of what you receive back to God is a way of honouring Him. Tithing was a law in the Old Testament, but in the New Testament, we're not under the law anymore. However, it's still a great practice to begin with. God loves a cheerful giver! And the important thing is that you're giving back to God first, not reluctantly, but out of love and gratitude. Then, the rest of the money—whether it's from gifts, your allowance, or a part-time job—should be used wisely. Set a budget for your needs, wants, and future goals."

Daughter: [Thoughtfully]

"So, 10% goes into savings and 10% to God? Is that what you mean by tithing?"

Mom:

"Exactly. You can use the tithe to support your church or a charity that you believe in. But the very important thing is that you're giving back to God first, before anything else. After that, you decide how to budget the rest of your money. Remember, it's all about balance."

How to Apply the Lesson Immediately:

Mom: [Looking directly at her kids]

"Now, let's talk about how you can apply this right now. Let's say you both get some money. [Daughter], maybe it's from a birthday, or [Son], maybe it's your allowance. Think about where that money is going."

Daughter: [Raises an eyebrow]

"Well, I usually spend my money on things like clothes or snacks at the mall."

Mom: [Nods]

"Okay, that's a great example. Now, what if you set aside 10% for God first? You can give that to the church or a cause you care about. Then, out of the remaining money, put aside a portion for savings—maybe for something like a new phone or your future. After that, you can budget for the fun stuff, but it's important to see how the priorities change when you follow these steps."

Son 1: [Looking thoughtful]

"I usually just spend whatever I get on games or hanging out with friends."

Mom:

"Right, and that's fine, but what if you saved up a little for something bigger—maybe a car when you get older or a very special trip? If you start practising budgeting now, you'll build habits that will serve you well in the future."

3. Giving: The Joy of Generosity
Mom:

"Let's talk about giving now. It's something that should be close to your hearts as Christians. In 2 Corinthians 9:7, it says, 'Each of you should give what you have decided in your heart to give, not reluctantly or under compulsion, for God loves a cheerful giver.' When you give, you're demonstrating that you trust God with your finances and also helping others in the process. It doesn't matter how much you give, but it's the heart behind it."

Son 1: [Thinking very sincerely]

"So, when we give, it's not just about money—it's about trusting God with what He's given us and sharing it?"

Mom:

"Exactly. Sometimes, giving might mean money, but it could also mean time or helping others in practical ways. It's not just about what's in your bank account, but what's in your heart."

4. Avoiding Debt and Living Within Your Means

Mom: [Leaning in, looking at both kids very seriously]

"Another big lesson is about debt. It's easy to get into debt these days with credit cards and loans. But the Bible warns us about the dangers of debt. In Proverbs 22:7, it says, 'The rich rule over the poor, and the borrower is slave to the lender.' Debt can keep you from being financially free and can cause a lot of stress."

Son 2: [Eyes wide]

"So, that means we should avoid getting into debt at all costs?"

Mom:

"Yes, it's best to live within your means. If you don't have enough money for something, don't go into debt to get it. **Mom [leaning forward a little, looking between them]:**

"You know, sometimes it's tempting to just get something right away, especially when everyone else seems to have it. But trust me—it's always better to wait and save up until you can really afford it.

Living *below* your means isn't about being stingy or missing out—it's actually a principle that will save you so much stress in the long run. Debt and financial pressure can wear on your peace of mind, and God doesn't want that for us. He wants us to be wise, to plan, and to live with freedom, not anxiety."

[Pause. She softens her tone even more, placing a hand gently on Binta's arm.]

"And one more thing—let's talk about work. Work isn't just a punishment from the fall or something we *have* to do to survive. God created work. He designed us to be productive, creative, and useful in the world. When you work—whether it's helping someone, starting a little business, or just doing your chores with care—you're not just earning; you're *honoring God* with your effort.

He blesses our work, not just for our own needs, but so we can also be a blessing to others. That's how He designed the rhythm of life. We receive, we give. We work, we rest. We earn, we share. It's a beautiful cycle when it's done in love." When you start earning money, whether from a part-time job or doing chores for others, you're learning the value of hard work."

Son 1: [Perking up, nodding]

"I've been thinking about getting a summer job when I'm older."

Mom:

"That's a very great idea. And when you start working, remember to give your best. Whether it's a small task or a big one, doing your best in everything reflects your relationship with God. Colossians 3:23 says, 'Whatever you do, work at it with all your heart, as working for the Lord, not for human masters.'"

6. Trusting God with Your Finances
Mom: [Softly, with warmth]

"At the end of the day, we trust God with our finances. When we give Him the first part of what we earn, when we manage what He's given us well, and when we choose to live within our means, we're honouring Him. Proverbs 3:9-10 says, 'Honor the Lord with your wealth, with the first fruits of all your crops; then your barns will be filled to overflowing, and your vats will brim over with new wine.'"

Daughter: [Smiling gently]

"I think I understand now. It's about being wise and giving back to God, but also taking care of what He gives us."

Son 1: [Nodding] "Yeah, and not getting too attached to money. It's just a tool."

Mom: [Nods, smiling very warmly and with pride]

"Exactly. You both are starting on the right foot. Following God's way isn't just about rules—it infuses wisdom into you. When you choose to follow His ways in everything, you grow wiser, and that's something you want to keep building on your whole life. Handling money very wisely is just one part of that. It's a skill that will serve you for the rest of your days. But the most important thing? Always keep God at the center of it all."

Son 2: [Grinning confidently]

"Thanks, Mom. I'm definitely going to start budgeting my allowance more carefully now!"

Mom: [Laughing softly, eyes twinkling]

"I'm proud of you both. And remember, we're all learning together. God's ways really are the best ways to follow—even when it comes to money or any part of life."

Mother's Teaching # 4 Teaching Your Teen Daughter to Move the Hand of God

Hannah had been guiding her daughter, Grace, in the art of prayer for a while now. Initially, Grace was sceptical—she found it difficult to believe that prayer could lead to real, tangible change. But as time passed, and with each prayer, a profound transformation took place. What started as a mere exercise became a powerful connection with God. Now, Grace understood that prayer wasn't just a list of requests—it was about drawing heaven's power down to earth. And with that understanding, she began to walk in greater confidence, knowing her prayers could move mountains.

Step 1: Align Your Requests with God's Word

Hannah began by teaching Grace, one of the most foundational principles of prayer: to base every request on what God has already said in His Word. "Remember, Grace," she would say, "God has already given us everything we need to know in the Bible. His Word is a guide, a blueprint for how to live and what to ask for. When you pray, make sure your requests align with what God has promised."

One evening, as they read through Psalm 44:1-3 together, Hannah pointed out how the psalmist recalled God's mighty acts of deliverance for previous generations. "This is what You did, God," she said, "and this is what we need today. When we pray, we remind God of His promises. We tap into what He has already said."

Grace's eyes lit up. It clicked for her—prayer wasn't about asking for random things or wishful thinking; it was about claiming what God had already promised. Each prayer was a powerful act of agreement with God's Word.

Step 2: Belief in God's Integrity

Hannah knew that for Grace to move the hand of God, she needed to trust in God's integrity fully. "Grace," she explained, "God cannot lie. When He says something, it *becomes*. His Word is truth, and He is faithful to what He has spoken. If He said it, you can trust He will bring it to pass."

Hannah would often remind Grace to declare God's promises with confidence in prayer. "God, I'm standing on Your Word because You cannot go back on it. I trust You to move on my behalf."

This wasn't about blind faith; it was rooted in the unshakable truth of who God is. Psalm 138:1-2 became one of Grace's favourite verses as Hannah explained that God's Word is magnified above His very name. "God is so faithful to His Word, He doesn't need to prove Himself—His Word stands as the final authority."

Step 3: Ask with a Heart. Prepared for the Answer

While teaching Grace, Hannah always emphasized the importance of a heart that was ready to meet God. "When you pray, don't just ask because it's a routine," she said. "Prepare your heart to meet with God truly. Be open to Him speaking, even when you can't immediately feel His presence. His silence isn't abandonment—it's an invitation to seek Him more."

Grace began to understand that prayer wasn't just about asking for things but about drawing close to God and trusting in His timing. Sometimes, answers didn't come right away, but that didn't mean God wasn't at work behind the scenes.

And when doubts or fears crept in, when the enemy tried to convince her that God didn't care or wouldn't show up, Hannah was there to remind her. "When the devil tries to make you question God's goodness or His willingness to answer, remember this: God is a person of integrity, and His Word *cannot* return void. Don't let the enemy steal your confidence." Hannah's unwavering support was a constant source of reassurance for Grace, strengthening her resolve in the face of doubt.

Step 4: Invoke God's Power with Confidence

As Grace grew in her understanding of prayer, Hannah encouraged her to pray with boldness. "God is not moved by fear or timidity. Your faith moves him," she would say. "When you pray, be specific. Just like the psalmist did in Psalm 80:1-3, don't just ask in vague terms. Be clear about what you're asking for, knowing that God hears you."

One night, Grace was struggling with peer pressure and bullying at school. She felt trapped and helpless. That evening, she poured her heart out in prayer. "God," she prayed, "just like You moved in the past to deliver Jacob, I need You to move for me now. Arise in my school and bring deliverance over my situation."

It wasn't a vague prayer. It was a prayer rooted in God's history of deliverance, patterned after the stories in the Bible that they had studied together. Within days, Grace began to notice changes—some friends who had been distant were now more open, and the bullying she had endured started to decrease.

Step 5: Stand on God's Word, No Matter What

Hannah's final lesson was one of perseverance and unwavering faith. "Grace, God's Word is settled in heaven," she explained, quoting Psalm 119:89. "When you pray, you're not begging God to change His mind. You're aligning yourself with His plan, which is already set."

By this point, Grace had seen the power of God's Word at work in her life, and she knew that prayer wasn't just about asking—it was about standing firm on the promises that God had already spoken. One afternoon, Hannah watched her daughter pray with quiet yet unshakable confidence, declaring, "I believe in God's Word. It's settled, and I'm standing on it."

A Testimony of God's Faithfulness

As Grace continued to practice these steps in her own life, she began to see even bigger answers to her prayers—answers for her family, her friends, and her future. She saw the power of prayer not only as a tool for asking but as a way to align with God's will and see His kingdom come on earth. This alignment gave her a sense of purpose and direction in her prayer life.

One evening, after a compelling prayer session, Grace turned to her mom with a bright smile. "Mom," she said, "I get it now. God's Word is all we need. I'm ready to pray with faith for even bigger things."

And with that, the legacy of faith continued—from mother to daughter. Through clear, step-by-step teaching, Hannah had shown Grace how to move the hand of God. And now, Grace was ready to walk in that authority and teach others to do the same.

Key Takeaways for Mothers Teaching Their Daughters to Pray

1. **Align Requests with God's Word**: Always base your prayers on what God has already promised in Scripture. This makes your prayer more effective and aligns it with His will.

2. **Believe in God's Integrity**: Trust that God will keep His promises. His Word is unbreakable, and His integrity ensures He will never fail you.

3. **Prepare Your Heart**: Prayer isn't a quick transaction—it's a relationship. Ensure that your heart is ready to hear from God and that you are open to His timing and ways.

4. **Pray with Confidence**: Speak boldly and specifically when asking God for help. Trust that He hears your prayers and will act according to His Word.

5. **Stand Firm on God's Promises**: When you pray, remember that God's Word is already settled in heaven. Trust that His promises will come to pass, and stand firm in faith, even when circumstances don't align with your expectations.

By following these steps, you can help your daughter not only understand how to pray but also teach her to believe in the power of prayer and see God move in her life. Through faith, trust, and persistence, your daughter will learn how to move the hand of God and become a powerful woman of prayer.

Mother's Teaching # 5: Teaching Your Daughter About Her Spiritual Womb

One evening, as the golden light from the setting sun gently filled the room, Grace sat in the corner, quietly reading her Bible. The air felt calm, but Hannah knew there was something on her heart that she needed to share—a lesson on prayer and God's purposes, something she had been practicing herself and wanted to pass on to her daughter.

"Grace," Hannah began, sitting down beside her, "can I share something important with you tonight?"

Grace looked up, her curiosity piqued. "Sure, Mom. What's on your heart?"

Hannah smiled, her eyes warm with love. "I want to talk to you about something special—how you, as a girl, have a spiritual womb. A place where God's purpose for your life grows."

Grace blinked, slightly confused. "A spiritual womb? What do you mean by that?"

Hannah took a deep breath, gently gathering her thoughts. "Well, let's start with something you know. When a woman is going to have a baby, the seed comes from the man, right? The woman doesn't have the seed—only the man does. The woman's job is to carry the seed and let it grow in her womb."

Grace nodded slowly, the wheels turning in her mind. "Okay, I understand that. The woman carries the baby in her womb, and it grows until it's time to be born."

"Exactly," Hannah said. "Now, just like that, you have a *spiritual womb* inside you. This is where God places His purpose for your life. He plants seeds of His dreams, His plans, His Word, and your spiritual womb holds them until they're ready to come to life."

Step 1: Understanding the Physical Womb

Hannah wanted to make sure Grace understood the natural concept first. "You see, Grace, the womb doesn't create the baby. The woman doesn't make the baby, but she plays a huge part by carrying and nurturing it. She protects it and lets it grow."

Grace thought about it for a moment. "So, the woman doesn't create the baby, but she helps it grow until it's ready to come out?"

"That's right," Hannah confirmed. "The womb is like an incubator—it holds the seed and gives it the perfect environment to grow into something beautiful. The woman cooperates with the process of bringing that life into the world."

Step 2: Your Spiritual Womb

Hannah leaned in, her tone soft but full of conviction. "Now, here's the powerful part, Grace. Just like a woman has a physical womb, you have a *spiritual womb*. This is where God places His seeds—His plans and His purpose for your life. When God speaks to you, whether through a promise, a calling, or a vision, He plants that seed in your spiritual womb. And just like the physical womb, you have to nurture it and protect it."

Grace's eyes widened with understanding. "So, God gives me His plans for my life, and it's my job to help them grow, just like a baby grows in the womb?"

"Exactly," Hannah said, her voice full of love and pride. "When God speaks to your heart, He plants His seeds—His Word, His promises. You might not see the full picture right away, but as you pray, worship, and trust Him, those seeds begin to grow. Your spiritual womb holds them until they're ready to come to life."

Step 3: Nurturing the Seed Through Prayer

Grace leaned forward, eager to learn more. "So, how do I take care of these seeds, Mom? How do I make them grow?"

Hannah smiled, happy to see Grace so engaged. "Well, just like a mother cares for her body while carrying a baby, you have to take care of your spiritual life. You nurture these seeds through prayer, worship, and meditating on God's Word. Your prayers are like the food the seeds need to grow strong."

"When you pray, you're feeding those seeds," Hannah continued. "You're giving them strength to grow and develop."

Grace's face lit up. "So, the more I pray and believe in God's promises, the stronger His plans for me become?"

"Yes, exactly!" Hannah said, her heart swelling with pride. "Every prayer you pray is like adding life to that seed. It's like watering a plant or feeding a baby—it nurtures God's plans for your future and helps them grow. Each time you pray, you're giving those promises the energy they need to take root and flourish in your life."

Step 4: Praying and Birthing God's Purpose

Grace leaned back in her chair, her mind racing with new thoughts. It felt like a whole new world of possibility had opened up to her. Prayer wasn't just about asking for things anymore—it was about partnering with God to bring His plans to life.

Hannah saw the shift in her daughter's expression and gently added, "Here's the next thing I want you to understand, Grace. God doesn't just want to plant seeds in your life—He wants you to *birth* them. Just like a woman gives birth to a baby after carrying it for months, you also have a part in bringing God's purposes into the world."

Grace blinked, taking it in. "So, I don't just pray for God's plans to grow in me, but I also pray for them to come into the world?"

"Exactly!" Hannah replied, her voice firm but filled with grace. "You're partnering with God in prayer to bring those seeds to life. You're standing in faith, even when things still seem small. Through your prayers, you help bring God's will into the world, just like a mother brings forth her child."

Step 5: Trusting the Timing

Grace's heart stirred with excitement. "So, when I pray for change in my school or for God to use me to help others, I'm helping bring His plans into reality?"

"Yes," Hannah replied, her eyes shining with confidence. "When you pray with faith, you're birthing God's plans into your generation. Your prayers matter, Grace. Never underestimate how much God can do through your faith and persistence."

Grace smiled, feeling both comforted and empowered. She had always known that prayer was important, but now she saw that her prayers weren't just for herself—they were a vital part of God's plan for the world.

Hannah smiled back. "Remember, sweetie, God's timing is always perfect. Just like a baby needs time to grow, God's plans for you need time to unfold. Things won't happen overnight, but if you stay faithful, God will bring those seeds to full bloom at the right time."

Grace nodded thoughtfully. "So, I just need to trust the timing?"

"Yes," Hannah said with a knowing smile. "God has a perfect timing for everything. Even if you don't see the fruit of your prayers right away, keep nurturing the seed. Keep praying, believing, and trusting in God. In time, you'll see His plans unfold."

Key Takeaways for Teaching Your Daughter About Her Spiritual Womb

1. **You Have a Spiritual Womb**: Just like a woman's womb carries and nurtures a baby, you have a spiritual womb where God plants His plans and purposes for your life. Your role is to carry, protect, and nurture these seeds until they come to life.

2. **Nurture God's Seeds Through Prayer**: Prayer is like food for the seeds God has planted in you. Through prayer, worship, and faith, you nurture God's plans for your future, giving them the strength to grow and thrive.

3. **Partner with God in Birthing His Purposes**: Your prayers don't just protect the seed—they help bring God's plans into the world. Just like a mother gives birth to a child, you partner with God to birth His purposes through prayer and faith.

4. **Trust the Timing**: Just like a baby takes time to grow, God's purposes in your life take time. Trust that God is working behind the scenes, preparing you for what's next. Stay faithful, and His plans will unfold in their perfect time.

By teaching Grace about her spiritual womb, Hannah helped her daughter see that prayer isn't just about asking for things—it's about partnering with God to bring His purposes into the world. Grace walked away from that conversation with a renewed sense of purpose, understanding that she had a vital role to play in God's kingdom and that her prayers were powerful enough to make a difference.

Mother's Teaching # 6: A Mother's Heartfelt Story

As a mother, there are few things as painful as watching your child stray from the path you've worked so hard to guide them along. I know this firsthand. My daughter, Lily, was once the picture of rebellion—nothing like the little girl I had prayed for, raised with care, and hoped would one day embrace the values I held dear. She became a teenager, and the changes were dramatic.

Lily wasn't just going through the usual teen mood swings. She was angry, defiant, and distant. The bright, caring girl I had known had transformed into someone I could hardly recognize. She started sneaking out, lying, cutting school, and hanging out with the wrong crowd. She'd ignore my calls and texts, stay out late, and when she did come home, it was as though she was in a different world—shut off from me, from everything I had taught her.

At first, I didn't know how to handle it. I felt betrayed, heartbroken, and helpless. But the one thing I did know was this: I could *pray*. I knew that God heard my cries, and He cared deeply about my daughter—about her heart, about her future. So I turned to Him, over and over again, sometimes in desperation, but always with faith that He would make a way.

What follows is the story of how God answered my prayers and helped me navigate the difficult path of raising a rebellious daughter. This is not a "quick fix" solution, but a journey that involves patience, faith, and relentless love. And while my journey with Lily was long and hard, I now stand in awe of the transformation she's undergone. After year 9, the girl who once rejected everything I said is now a compassionate, faithful young woman, ready to face life with the confidence of someone who knows her worth in Christ.

Step 1: Seek God's Wisdom in Prayer (Before You React)

In the early stages of Lily's rebellion, I didn't always know how to respond. It was tempting to shout, demand answers, or punish her into submission. But I quickly realized that my frustration and anger weren't the answers. Instead, I took everything to prayer.

What I Did:

- I spent hours in prayer, asking God for wisdom in how to handle each situation.
- I prayed for Lily's heart to be softened, for the Holy Spirit to intervene, and for me to have the patience to listen and understand her.

- I prayed that God would surround her with people who could influence her positively, even if I couldn't.

- I asked God for the strength to love Lily *through* her rebellion, even when it was hard.

Why It Worked:
Prayer became my lifeline. I could feel the Lord's peace even in the middle of the storm. He guided me to show compassion rather than condemnation, and He slowly started working on Lily's heart—even when I didn't see the change right away.

Scripture to Encourage Moms:
"If any of you lacks wisdom, let him ask of God, who gives to all liberally and without reproach, and it will be given to him."
— *James 1:5*

Step 2: Set Boundaries, But Love Unconditionally
Lily was testing boundaries constantly. She would break curfew, defy my rules, and sometimes even lie straight to my face. There were days I felt like I was losing control. But in those moments, I knew I had to stand firm in the boundaries I set, even if it meant facing her anger.

What I Did:
- I consistently set clear, firm boundaries: curfews, rules about friendships, consequences for skipping school, and expectations around respect. There was no wavering, even when she tried to push back.

- I let her know that my love for her was not conditional on her behavior, but my authority as her mother still stood.

- When she did something rebellious, I didn't react with fury but instead calmly explained why her actions were wrong and how they affected her future.

Why It Worked:
Lily often tested my boundaries, but over time, she started to respect them because they were consistent and rooted in love. It wasn't always immediate, but I could see that she valued the stability and protection that boundaries offered, even if she didn't express it at the time.

Scripture to Encourage Moms:
"Train up a child in the way he should go, and when he is old, he will not depart from it." — **Proverbs 22:6**

Step 3: Encourage Open Communication, Even Through the Silence
There were so many times when Lily wouldn't speak to me. She'd shut herself in her room, or we'd have conversations that felt like talking to a brick wall. But I had to keep trying. I had to show her that no matter what, I was *here*—listening, caring, and available.

What I Did:
- I created spaces for calm, non-confrontational conversations. Even if it was just 5 minutes here and there, I made it clear I was available to listen when she was ready.

- I didn't press too hard, but I didn't let her silence push me away. I would simply ask how her day was, express concern without criticism, and let her know I loved her no matter what.

- I validated her feelings. Instead of getting defensive, I listened. "I can see you're upset. What's going on, honey?" This helped her feel understood and less alienated.

Why It Worked:
Over time, Lily began to open up. It wasn't instant, but by remaining patient and consistent, she began to trust that I was safe to talk to. Gradually, our communication became more open and honest, and I could begin to understand what was going on in her heart.

Scripture to Encourage Moms:
"Let your conversation be always full of grace, seasoned with salt, so that you may know how to answer everyone."
— Colossians 4:6

Step 4: Don't Let Her Rebellion Define Her Identity—Remind Her of Who She Is
During the rebellious years, I often saw Lily lost in her identity. She was influenced by the wrong crowd, trying to fit in with friends who didn't have her best interests at heart. But I refused to let her mistakes define who she was in God's eyes.

What I Did:
- I consistently reminded Lily of her value in Christ. I would pray over her at night, speaking God's truth over her, even when I felt like she wasn't listening.
- I used moments of quiet to remind her of the young woman God was calling her to be—kind, strong, intelligent, and beautiful.

- I didn't allow the enemy to whisper lies about her. Even in the hardest moments, I would speak encouragement, calling forth the greatness within her.

Why It Worked:
The power of speaking life over her was transformative. Slowly, Lily began to internalize the truth of her identity—not from her friends, her mistakes, or even her own fears—but from God. She started to realize she didn't have to act out to prove her worth.

Scripture to Encourage Moms:
"I have loved you with an everlasting love; I have drawn you with unfailing kindness." — **Jeremiah 31:3**

Step 5: Don't Give Up—Keep Praying
Even in the darkest moments, when it felt like nothing was changing, I knew I couldn't give up. I had to keep praying, keep trusting, and keep loving. It wasn't easy. Some days I doubted. But God's faithfulness was never in question.

What I Did:
- I stayed in prayer for Lily every day—praying for her heart, for her friends, for her future. I prayed for God to soften her heart and remove the destructive influences in her life.

- I never stopped speaking life into her. Even when she was ungrateful, rebellious, or silent, I refused to stop loving her unconditionally.

- I found support from other moms in prayer groups, sharing my burdens and receiving strength in unity.

Why It Worked:

After year 9, I began to see changes. Slowly but surely, Lily started to come around. She made better choices, started hanging out with a more positive group of friends, and, most importantly, she began to seek God for herself. By the time she was 16, Lily had transformed. She was a responsible, thoughtful, and loving young woman. I could see that the years of prayer and consistent love had shaped her into someone I was proud of.

Scripture to Encourage Moms:

"The prayer of a righteous person is powerful and effective."
— *James 5:16*

Conclusion:

The Power of Prayer and Unwavering Love

Lily is now a confident, grounded young woman, with a heart full of compassion for others. She's actively involved in church, has a strong sense of her identity in Christ, and is becoming the young woman I always knew she could be. I can't say it was easy, but I can say it was worth it. Through prayer, patience, and unconditional love, God did what I couldn't do on my own.

To all the moms who are struggling with rebellious teens—don't give up. Keep praying, keep loving, and trust that God is working, even when you can't see it. Your faithfulness will bear fruit, and in time, you will see the transformation you've been praying for.

Mother's Teaching # 7: A Mother's Journey — Teaching Sibling Harmony and Overcoming Rivalry

Introduction: The Battle of Sibling Rivalry

As a mother, you'll know that sibling rivalry is one of those things that feels like it will never end. The bickering, the fighting, the jealous glances, and the tears—it can feel like a constant battle. But what's really tricky is how easy it is to get pulled into the chaos, trying to referee every disagreement, wondering if you're doing something wrong as a parent. I've been there, trust me.

My four kids—Sam (the oldest), Elijah (the middle child), Zoe (the second oldest), and Mia (the youngest)—have all had their fair share of moments where they were either competing for my attention or arguing about who's the "best" at something. There were times when Sam, the firstborn, felt like he had to lead, sometimes a bit too much, pushing his siblings around.

Elijah, the middle child, would feel overlooked, as if he was neither the baby nor the oldest, trying to find his place. Zoe, just a little older than Mia, often struggled with feeling stuck between two worlds—wanting to be the older sister but still craving attention. And Mia, the baby, well, she often felt both adored and suffocated—loved but a little too pampered.

At the beginning, I was constantly stepping in to manage their rivalry, trying to balance attention, trying to make sure no one felt left out. It was overwhelming. But over time, I realized that sibling rivalry, although very tough, doesn't have to be the enemy. It's an opportunity to teach them about love, respect, and most importantly, how to build each other up, not tear each other down. Here's what I learned that changed the way I approach sibling relationships—and how you can, too.

Step 1: Understand the Roots of Rivalry – Why It Happens
The first thing I had to accept was that sibling rivalry is **normal**. It's part of growing up. When you're raising kids with different personalities and different stages of development, there's bound to be some tension. And that's okay. It's not a sign that you're failing as a mom. It's just a part of family life.

Here's what I learned about my kids:

- **Sam, the oldest**, sometimes felt the weight of being "the leader." He'd try to boss around his siblings or, at times, get frustrated when he didn't get as much freedom as Elijah, who was younger. It wasn't that he was being mean, it was just that he was trying to navigate what it meant to be the oldest.

- **Elijah, the middle child**, often felt like the "forgotten" one. He wasn't the baby, and he wasn't the firstborn. He didn't get the very privileges of being the youngest, but also didn't have the responsibilities that Sam did. This sometimes led him to act out for attention.

- **Zoe, the second oldest**, found herself stuck between being the "older" sibling and still wanting to be treated like the baby sometimes. She was also the bridge between Sam and Mia, and she often felt like she had to play a balancing role. But this sometimes led to frustration.

- **Mia, the youngest**, was often the one who felt both spoiled and suffocated at the same time. While everyone adored her, she also didn't get the same amount of freedom her siblings did, which left her feeling trapped.

The key takeaway here is that sibling rivalry often arises when needs aren't met—whether it's attention, validation, or simply the recognition of their unique role in the family. Once I understood that, I didn't see their struggles as failures but as natural growth pains.

Step 2: Encourage Healthy Competition and Comparison with Jesus
This is where things got a little tricky for me as a mom. How do you teach kids not to compete with each other? How do you get them to stop comparing themselves to their siblings, or worse, feeling inferior because they're not "as good" as someone else?

I had to help them realize something really important: **comparison is a thief**—it steals your peace, your joy, and your sense of worth.

I remember one day, Sam came to me, frustrated. "Why can't I be as smart as Elijah? Why is everything so easy for him?" And Zoe would complain, "Mia gets away with everything!" It was clear that my children were measuring themselves against each other—and always coming up short. The key moment came when I shared with them an important lesson that has stuck with them ever since:

God didn't create you to be like your siblings. He created you to be like Jesus.

We often talk about how God made mankind in His image (Genesis 1:26-27), but when I really stopped to think about it, I realized something profound. **God made animals in their own image, plants in their image, but He made man in His image**. A lion can say to another lion, you are doing well because they have the same image, but only God can tell you how you are doing because we are created in his image and this is the purpose of final judgement. But here's the kicker: as Christians, we are meant to **reflect the image of Jesus**, not anyone else unless they are also following the image.

When you compare yourself to a sibling, to a friend, or to a classmate, you're measuring yourself against something temporary. But when you compare yourself to **Jesus**, you're looking at the perfect standard. **Jesus is the only image we're called to reflect**, and if that's our goal—if that's the image we strive toward—then we'll always have room to grow, but in a way that fills us with grace, not insecurity.

I told my kids, "Don't compare yourself to Sam, don't compare yourself to Zoe or Mia—compare yourself to Jesus. When you look at Him, you'll see how far you need to go, and it won't make you feel bad about yourself. It'll make you realize that you can be more like Him every single day. And when you fall short, He'll be there with grace."

Step 3: Teach Conflict Resolution

One thing I learned early on is that **conflict isn't the enemy**—it's how you handle it that counts. Kids are going to fight, argue, and have their moments of tension. But if we can help them resolve those very conflicts in a healthy way, they'll learn valuable skills for life.

What I did:

- I set up **"Family Meetings"** where everyone had a chance to speak openly about what was bothering them. No yelling. No interrupting. Just listening. It helped the kids feel heard, and we all learned how to express our feelings calmly.

- We worked on using **"I" statements** to express ourselves without blaming. Instead of, "You always take my stuff," we practiced saying, "I feel upset when my things are taken without asking."

- And sometimes, we even did some role-playing, acting out different conflicts to work through solutions.

By encouraging open communication, I saw the kids move from fighting to solving problems together.

Step 4: Encourage Empathy and Compassion
One of the best things I did was teach my kids to see the world through each other's eyes. Empathy is key to sibling harmony.

What I did:

- I'd share times when Sam might feel overwhelmed by responsibility, or when Zoe felt stuck in the middle. We talked about how Mia might crave more independence but feel like the baby of the family.

- I encouraged acts of kindness. Whether it was Sam helping Zoe with homework, or Mia giving Elijah her last cookie, I made sure to praise these moments. They weren't just "being nice," they were learning how to love like Jesus does.

Step 5: Celebrate Unity
Finally, I made sure to celebrate when things went right. Whether it was Sam finally letting Elijah pick the movie, or Zoe supporting Mia in a tough moment, we celebrated those moments of unity.

The rewards were very tangible: the kids began to realize that working together as a family was much more fulfilling than competing with each other.

Final Thoughts:

As a mom, I've learned that **sibling rivalry** doesn't have to tear your family apart. It's an opportunity to teach love, empathy, forgiveness, and, most importantly, how to reflect **Jesus**. Every time we focus on growing into His image, we set aside our competition and comparisons and start becoming more like Him—together.

And trust me, you'll get there. One moment at a time as you renew you mind with His word.

Scripture to Encourage Moms:
"Do nothing from selfish ambition or conceit, but in humility count others more significant than yourselves."
— Philippians 2:3

Mother's Teaching # 8: A Mother's Heartfelt Talk with Ella: Embracing Your Unique Beauty & Navigating the Pressure of Relationships

It was another quiet evening at home. The glow from Ella's phone illuminated her face as she scrolled through Instagram, pausing every so often to stare at photos of couples—holding hands, hugging, and sharing what seemed like perfect moments. Her mom, Maria, entered the room and noticed the heaviness in her daughter's eyes.

Mom (Maria): *gently sitting beside Ella* "Hey, honey, what's going on? You've been really quiet tonight."

Ella: *sighing deeply, avoiding her mom's gaze* "It's just... all the girls at school. They're all in relationships. Every single one of them. They have boys who tell them they're beautiful, who take them out, who hold their hands in the hallways. And... I don't even know if I'll ever have that. It's like I'm invisible, Mom. No guy has ever even told me he likes me, let alone loved me. I don't even think I'm capable of that. What's wrong with me?"

Mom (Maria): *softly rubbing Ella's back* "Oh, baby, I know it's hard. I hear you, and I see the pain in your eyes. You feel like everyone else is moving forward in their relationships, and you're still on the sidelines. It's easy to feel like something's wrong with you when you don't fit into the mold everyone else seems to be in."

Maria pauses, choosing her words very carefully.

"But let me tell you something that might sound a little different from what the world tells you."

Step 1: The Truth About Relationships and Timing

Mom (Maria): *gently* "You know, honey, everyone's story is different. Just because all the girls at school have boyfriends doesn't mean that you're behind. What if—just *what if*—God has a perfect time for you? A time where you'll meet the right person who will see you for who you are—inside and out—and love you for it?"

Ella: *scoffing a little* "But Mom, all the other girls have guys who call them pretty and take them out. They're not waiting around for 'the right time.' They're living their lives. And I'm over here wondering if anyone will ever even *notice* me."

Mom (Maria): *nodding with understanding* "I get it, I really do. It's frustrating. But sometimes, what the world offers—the quick relationships, the shallow compliments—aren't what your heart needs. Do you know that? You might be feeling left out now, but I promise, there's someone out there who's going to appreciate every bit of you—your heart, your soul, your personality. And the best part is, *you won't have to change a thing to fit their idea of what 'love' is supposed to look like.*"

Step 2: You Are Not Invisible—You Are Waiting for Something Real

Mom (Maria): "The truth is, Ella, I don't want you to settle for anything less than the best. Relationships in school? They can be fleeting. They can be based on appearances, on who's popular, who fits into a mold. But when you are loved by someone, it will be about so much more than what you look like on the outside."

Ella tilts her head, still unconvinced but listening intently.

"You are not invisible. You are just *waiting* for someone who will see you for everything you are—and that's not something that happens overnight. I want you to know, no boy has the right to define your worth. It's not about *being chosen*—it's about *knowing your worth* and then allowing someone to *recognize it and appreciate it*."

Step 3: God's Timing and Your Uniqueness—A Relationship With Purpose

Mom (Maria): *smiling gently* "In the Bible, God tells us that He has a perfect plan for our lives, even in relationships. **Jeremiah 29:11** says, *'For I know the plans I have for you,' declares the Lord, 'plans to prosper you and not to harm you, plans to give you a hope and a future.'* That includes your future relationships, Ella. He knows exactly when and how it's meant to happen."

Maria looks at Ella with loving eyes.

"I know it feels like everyone else is moving ahead, but maybe, just maybe, God is waiting for you to grow into the woman He's designed you to be before He brings the right person into your life. Maybe He wants to show you how to love yourself first, without needing anyone else's validation, before you find someone who will truly value you."

Ella: *quietly* "But, what if I'm too late? What if I miss out on love because I'm not like everyone else? What if I'm meant to be alone forever?"

Step 4: You Are Beautiful, Loved, and Worthy of Real Love

Mom (Maria): *looking at her daughter with a deep, knowing gaze* "Ella, I want you to listen to me. The way you feel right now—thinking that love is just about being with someone else—is a lie the world tells you. You are already loved. God's love is always there for you, no matter what. **Romans 8:38-39** says, *'For I am convinced that neither death nor *life, neither angels nor demons, neither the present nor the future, nor any powers, neither height nor depth, nor anything else in all creation, will be able to separate us from the love of God that is in Christ Jesus our Lord.'* Do you hear that? No one can take away the love God has for you. You are already loved *completely* by Him."

Ella's eyes fill with tears as she absorbs her mom's words.

Mom (Maria): "You are enough, Ella. More than enough. And I know it hurts now, especially when you look around and see everyone else getting attention. But real love? It's more than a high school crush. It's about being seen for who you truly are, for all of the goodness inside of you. You deserve someone who will love you for your kindness, your heart, your unique qualities—*not just your appearance.*"

Step 5: The Waiting Doesn't Define You—You Define You

Mom (Maria): *sitting back, thoughtful* "I want to tell you something else, something that might be hard to hear but is incredibly important. Being in a relationship doesn't complete you. You are already complete in Christ, Ella. When you *know* your worth—when you love yourself, body and soul, just as you are—that's when you'll be ready for a relationship that's healthy, lasting, and God-ordained. Until then, focus on the things that bring you joy, the things that make you grow as a person—because the more you grow in confidence and self-love, the more attractive you will be to the right person."

Ella wipes her eyes, taking in what her mom says.

Mind-Bending Thought for Ella (and all Teen Girls Feeling the Pressure)

Mom (Maria): *leaning in, her voice soft but firm* "Here's something I want you to really think about. What if the way you see your body—your shape, your size—isn't the most important thing in the world?

What if God created you exactly the way He wanted you to be, and that's where your true beauty lies? The world will try to tell you that you need to change, shrink, or become something else to be loved. But I want to flip that idea on its head."

Ella looks at her mom, her mind spinning a little.

"What if you were to believe that your true beauty—the one that is real, lasting, and unshakable—comes from within? What if that beauty, that strength, is what draws people to you? And when the right person comes along, they'll see you and say, 'Wow, you are the one I've been waiting for,' not because you changed yourself, but because you've become the *best version of you.*"

Key Takeaways for Ella and Teen Girls Who Feel Left Out or Invisible in Relationships:

1. **Timing is everything.** God has a perfect plan for your relationships. The right person will come at the right time—not because you fit someone else's standards, but because they see you for who you really are.

2. **Your worth isn't defined by someone else's love.** You are already loved by God, fully and completely. That love is unshakable, and no relationship can ever replace it.

3. **Real love is about recognizing who you are.** When you love yourself for who you truly are, you're setting the stage for a relationship built on respect, love, and admiration—not just appearances.

4. **Don't rush into relationships.** Focus on becoming the best version of yourself. The right person will love you for who you are—not who you try to be.

5. **You are complete in Christ.** You don't need anyone to complete you. You're already whole in Him.

Ella: *smiling, her heart a little lighter* "Thanks, Mom. I think I needed to hear that more than I realized."

Mom (Maria): *hugging Ella tightly* "I'll always be here for you, sweetheart. You are never invisible

Mother's Teaching #9: Fasting, Grace, and the Transformative Power of Peace in Parenting

It was one of those quiet afternoons when Sandra's mother felt the weight of a conversation that had been on her heart for a while. The sunlight was soft, and the world outside seemed at peace. It was the perfect time for a mother-daughter chat about something Sandra had been learning—something that would not only transform her but could help her friends, too.

Mother: *"Sandra, honey, I want to talk about something important today. I've noticed how you've been handling your words and actions lately. You've grown, especially in how you used to talk too much. Do you remember what that was like?"*

Sandra: *"Oh, I do! I used to talk all the time—like if there was a moment of silence, I had to fill it. I never realized how much I was doing it until recently."*

Mother: *"Yes, and I think I know why. You see, fasting has a special way of teaching us how to silence the noise in our hearts. When we fast, we're not just skipping a meal or two; we're also abstaining from food for a specified period. We're intentionally starving our flesh—those urges to talk too much, to react impulsively, or to give in to any weakness of the body."*

Sandra: *"Wait... so, fasting isn't just about food? It's about quieting the flesh?"*

Mother: *"Exactly. When you fast, you're telling your flesh, 'You don't get the control. My spirit is in charge now.' All those distractions—your emotions, your impulses—lose their grip. And once your flesh is weak, you're better able to hear from God. When we pray after fasting, it's like we have a clearer line to God. Our prayers have more power. And we're more in control of what's going on around us. The environment can't sway us as easily."*

Sandra: *"So, fasting helps me focus on what matters, and prayer gives me strength not to let the world drag me around?"*

Mother: *"Yes, sweetheart. You're creating space for grace. When the flesh is weak, the spirit becomes strong. You begin to speak with more grace, even in tough situations. You stop reacting to everything that's happening around you, and instead, you stand firm in peace. That's what I've seen in you very lately. You're learning to control your words, your emotions, and your thoughts. You're not so easily swayed anymore."*

Sandra: *"I think I get it. It's like when I'm fasting, the urge to over-talk is gone. It's like God fills that space instead, and I don't feel the need to control everything with my words."*

For *instance, Lily, who was struggling with her parents' arguments, found peace and strength through fasting and prayer. She was able to stay calm and very focused, even in the midst of chaos, and her relationship with her parents improved as a result."*

Sandra nodded, her face clouding over as she thought about her friend.

Sandra: *"Yes, Lily's been quiet lately. She told me that when her parents argue, it feels like a dark cloud is hanging over her head. She said it's like a demon is sitting on her head, controlling her thoughts. And the worst* part is that her dad has to go away to pray to calm the tension down. It's cumbersome for her."

Mother: "Poor thing. It breaks my heart. You know, Sandra, when parents argue, it's not just between them only. The kids feel it, too. Especially as they get older. When parents argue, kids start to feel like they're on unstable ground. It's like they're walking on eggshells, unsure of what might happen next which is not a good place to be. As kids, they may shut it out when they're younger, but when they're teens, it starts to affect them more very deeply. It disorients them. It makes them feel like their foundation is shaking."

Sandra: "That's so sad. I don't think Lily knows how to handle it. I can tell she's bothered by it, but she doesn't want to be the one to speak up."

Mother: "She doesn't need to speak up about the arguments, but she does need to find peace within herself. Lily has to remember that her parents' issues aren't hers to solve. She can't carry that weight. But she can pray. She can fast, like you've learned, and ask God to help her hold her peace, no matter what chaos is around her."

Sandra: "So, you think she should fast, too?"

Mother: "Yes. Fasting would help her overcome her feelings of being overwhelmed by her parents' emotions. It would give her strength to stay calm in the middle of it all. And when she prays, she's inviting God to fill the space where her anxiety used to be. It's not about controlling the situation but controlling herself. It's about inviting God's peace into her heart so the chaos doesn't overwhelm her."

Sandra: "I'm going to talk to her, Mum. I think she needs to hear this."

Mother: "I'm so proud of you, Sandra. You've lived this. You've experienced how fasting and prayer can bring peace. You've learned that, *even amid struggle, you don't have to argue or lose your peace. You have to trust God to hold you steady."*

Sandra: *"I get it now. I used to think fasting was only about food, but it's really about giving my flesh no power over me and letting God's grace take over. That's when I feel at peace."*

Mother: *"That's it, sweetheart. Fasting is about quieting your flesh and inviting God's presence into the space where noise used to be. And for Lily, for anyone, when you fast and pray, you're creating an environment of peace in your heart. And when your heart is at peace, the world around you can't shake you."*

The conversation between Sandra and her mother was a turning point—not just for Sandra, but for her understanding of how fasting can affect every area of her life. Sandra hadn't always been the calm in the storm. There were days when her words flew faster than her thoughts, and her reactions lit fires she didn't mean to start. But something shifted during her time of fasting. Slowly, quietly, she began to change—not just on the surface, but deep down where grace grows roots.

Fasting didn't just quiet her appetite—it quieted her spirit. She found herself breathing more, pausing longer, choosing peace over pride. It wasn't easy, but it was worth it. And people noticed.

The grace she'd received—grace to stay silent when angry, to speak gently when challenged, to love when she could have judged—became a light others could feel. Her home grew more peaceful. Her children leaned in more. And her friends, like Lily, came to her not just for advice—but for calm.

Now it was Sandra's turn to pour out what had been poured into her. When Lily showed up, overwhelmed and on edge, Sandra didn't rush to fix it. She just sat, listened, and let her presence be an anchor. She knew what it was like to feel frayed. But she also knew what it felt like to be held steady.

Through her own quiet transformation, Sandra had become a carrier of peace. Not because she never got very flustered—but because she'd learned how to bring every storm back to stillness.

Parents, Take Note:

As parents, it's easy to forget the impact our arguments can have on our children. When we fight, it doesn't just stay between us—it deeply affects our kids, especially as they grow older. The constant tension, the unresolved conflicts, the emotional rollercoaster—it leaves them disoriented and very vulnerable. And when kids are disoriented, they struggle to find their peace.

Fasting and prayer can be a powerful tool for parents to regain control over their emotions, quiet their flesh, and let God's peace reign in the home. When we take the time to fast and pray, we are not just changing ourselves—we are creating an environment of peace in which our children can grow.

If you're feeling overwhelmed, if your home is filled with tension, it might be time to step back and consider fasting—not just from food, but from the things that stir up conflict in your heart. And for your children, teaching them the power of fasting and prayer will help them hold onto peace amid turmoil.

Just like Sandra and her mother, we can all learn to turn to God, quiet our flesh, and let grace take over. That's the lesson that can change not only your life but the lives of those around you.

Mother's Teaching #10: Hearing the Voice of God

The late afternoon sun streamed through the living room curtains, casting warm rays across the wooden floor. A bible lay open on the coffee table, worn and underlined in many places—a clear testimony of years of use. Beside it sat Mama Ruth, a gentle yet firm woman in her fifties, her hair wrapped in a colourful scarf, her eyes deep with wisdom. Her daughter, Binta, a curious and lively teenager, nestled beside her, notebook in hand.

Mama Ruth began, her voice calm but rich with conviction:

"Binta, hearing the voice of God is not mystical. It's practical. The more you get used to the voice of scripture, the easier it is to recognize when God speaks. That's why you must read your Bible daily, underline the words, and meditate on them. That's how you train your Spirit."

Binta tilted her head, thoughtful. "But Mama, how do I know it's God speaking and not just... me thinking?"

Mama Ruth smiled, "That's a good question. When you're familiar with the Word of God, anything that doesn't align with it immediately stands out. If a voice brings lust, pride, or self-exaltation—it's not God. Satan's voice always carries a subtle seduction with it. He speaks to desire—but pushes it beyond God's boundaries."

Binta looked away for a moment, a shadow crossing her features. "I used to think differently," she admitted. "I used to think that if it feels right, it must be okay. I had a philosophy... a kind of lens that shaped everything I wanted and how I saw things. I now realize that was lust disguised as freedom."

Mama Ruth nodded knowingly. "Lust is not just about sex, my daughter. It's any desire that refuses to be governed by the Word of

God. The desire might be legitimate—like love, success, even sex in marriage—but when that desire doesn't submit to God's authority, it becomes lust. Satan uses that to lead us away."

There was silence between them for a moment. Then, **Binta's face lit up**—a spark of realization glowing in her eyes. "So when I pray now, and a scripture rises in my heart… that's the Holy Spirit, right?"

"Yes, child," Mama Ruth said, placing a gentle hand on her shoulder. "That's a sign you're spiritually healthy. When you pray, and scripture flows back, it shows you've stored His Word in your heart. The Holy Spirit pulls it up to guide you in real-time. That's an inspiration."

Binta leaned forward, excited. "It happened yesterday! I was feeling overwhelmed, and 'Be still and know that I am God' came to me so very clearly. It calmed me instantly."

Mama Ruth chuckled, "That's it! That's the voice of God—scripture applied at the right moment. Now contrast that with what the world calls 'enlightenment'. It's clever talk without submission to God. A kind of knowledge that sounds good but lacks truth. It's bondage disguised as freedom."

Binta nodded slowly. "Enlightenment tries to replace inspiration. But inspiration is from the Spirit—alive and exact."

"You see, Binta," Mama Ruth said, her tone gentle but firm, "every voice that comes into your 'garden'—your heart—must be weighed. Does it align with the Word? Does it submit to God's authority? If not, it's not of Him."

There was a long pause as Binta absorbed her mother's words. She glanced at the Bible on the table, then at her notebook, and quietly underlined a verse she had written earlier: *"Your word is a lamp unto my feet and a light unto my path."*

"Mama, I want to hear God. I want to study His Word—not just read it. I want to underline it, memorize it, live by it. I believe in the transformative power of His Word, and I want to experience it fully."

Her eyes lifted to meet her mother's. "You see, Mama, the devil's theatre of performance is the mind—where doubt thrives. But God's theatre of performance is the heart, where faith resides. What is in the mind cannot save you when the day of trouble comes; only what is hidden in the heart will. That's why we hide the Word in our hearts. It's not enough for it to just be in our minds. It must take root in our hearts, where it can truly transform us."

Mama Ruth smiled, her heart very full. "That's how it begins, my child. Not with a shout but with a whisper. Not with a crowd, but in quiet moments like this. Keep feeding your Spirit, and soon, God's voice will be as familiar as mine."

Lesson Summary – Mama's Teaching #10: Hearing the Voice of God

- The voice of God is recognized by those who are familiar with scripture.

- Reading and underlining the *physical Bible* helps develop spiritual hearing.

- Any desire that doesn't acknowledge the authority of God's Word becomes lust.

- Lust is not always evil in form, but it rebels against divine boundaries.

- Satan speaks by amplifying legitimate desires beyond God's limits.

- Enlightenment, without the Holy Spirit, becomes bondage disguised as wisdom.

- Inspiration from the Holy Spirit often comes through scripture in prayer.
- Spiritual health is evident when scripture rises in the heart during prayer.

Final Word from Mama Ruth:
"Child, the more you recognize the voice of scripture, the more you'll be trained to recognize the voice of the Shepherd."

Teaching #11: "From Anxious to Anchored: How to Replace Fear with Faith"

A mum's Heart-to-Heart Toolkit for Raising Resilient Christian Teens

Story-Driven Introduction: The Kitchen Table Moment

The hum of the dishwasher fills the kitchen, but the house feels tense. Your 15-year-old daughter, Emma, picks at her food, her eyes glassy, shoulders slumped. You've seen that look—it's the quiet storm of anxiety building up.

You pull out a chair beside her and gently brush her hair behind her ear.

"Hey, love... looks like your brain's on overdrive. Want to talk about it?"

She shrugs, hesitant—but the worry spills out:

"Mum... I've got this choir solo next week. I can't breathe when I think about it. My hands shake, I blank out... I know I'll mess up, everyone will laugh, I'll be the failure of the school."

Her words rush like a flood—familiar to every parent who's watched anxiety swallow their child whole.

The Teaching Moment: Replacing Anxiety with Faith

You breathe in, steady—this is the moment to anchor her, not with clichés, but absolute, biblical truth wrapped in love.

"Emma, I get it. Your fear feels huge right now. But Jesus knew we'd face these moments. Remember Matthew 6? He says, 'Take no thought for your life'—that means don't let anxious thoughts run wild. Worry sneaks in when we 'take' those thoughts and believe them as facts."

You lean closer, making it a more personal gesture.

"Anxiety tricks you into surrendering before anything's even happened. It shows you your weaknesses—makes you believe they define you."

Positive Example: Sarah's Story (A Teen Who Found Victory)

"Your cousin Sarah used to feel the same before her GCSEs. Her stomach knotted up; her palms got sweaty, and she was convinced she'd fail. But she learned to flip the script—every anxious thought became a prayer."

'God, I'm scared. But You've got me.'

"She prayed, she studied, and you know what? She still felt very nervous—but she didn't freeze. She took that test, one question at a time, because her heart was anchored."

Negative Example: Daniel's Story (A Teen Who Let Anxiety Win)

"Then there's Daniel. Same fear, different outcome. He let anxiety talk louder than faith. He skipped rehearsals, avoided class, and withdrew from his friends. He missed his shot, and the regret hit harder than the fear ever could."

Step-by-Step: Anchoring Your Teen Against Anxiety

Step 1: Recognise the Lie
The first thing is to spot those anxious thoughts when they creep in. It might sound like:

> *"I'll fail. I'll look stupid. Everyone will laugh."*

Pause right there. Label those thoughts for what they are—fear, not truth. That's the first way anxiety loses its grip on you.

Step 2: Reason with God's Word
Once you've called out the lie, replace it with God's promises. Speak truth over fear. For example:

> *"God's got good plans for me."* **(Jeremiah 29:11)**

When your teen learns to reason with scripture, their faith starts to rise above fear. This reliance on scripture can bring reassurance and confidence in the face of anxiety.

Step 3: Pray the Fear Out
Anxiety feeds on silence. So open your mouth and pray—even if your voice shakes. It can be very simple: "Jesus, I'm anxious. Give me Your peace." Turning panic into prayer invites God into the moment and weakens the power of fear. Remember, prayer is a powerful tool that can bring hope and empowerment in the face of anxiety.

> *"Jesus, I'm anxious. Give me Your peace." when you call on Him, he comes.*

Turning panic into prayer invites God into the moment and weakens the power of fear.

Step 4: Receive God's Very Peace
After you have prayed, breathe. Let God's peace settle in you. Picture it like a very strong, invisible armour wrapping your heart and mind—protecting you from anxious thoughts that wants to go in.

Step 5: Walk Daily in Peace
This isn't a one-time thing—it's daily. Build habits that anchor your faith. Simple things like a 3-minute morning prayer or whispering affirmations like: "God's with me. I can handle this." Little by little, those moments stack up, and peace becomes your new normal. Remember, it's the consistency of these daily habits that will lead to a more peaceful and anchored life.

"God's with me. I can handle this."

Little by little, those moments stack up, and peace becomes your new normal.

Step-by-Step: Anchoring Your Teen Against Anxiety

1.Step
Recognise the Lie

Action
Spot anxious thoughts

Example in Teen Life
'I'll fail, I'll look stupid'—Label them: *"That's fear, not truth."*

2. Step
Reason with God's Word

Action
Replace lies with promises

Example in Teen Life
'God's got good plans for me.' (Jeremiah 29:11)

3. Step
Pray the Fear Out

Action
Turn panic into prayer

Example in Teen Life
'Jesus, I'm anxious. Give me Your peace.'

4. Step
Receive God's Peace

Action
Let peace guard your mind

Example in Teen Life
Imagine peace as armour—your heart protected.

5. Step
Walk Daily in Peace

Action
Build habits that anchor faith

Example in Teen Life
3-min morning prayers, whispered affirmations.

Q&A: Real Questions, Real Help

Q: What if my child says prayer doesn't work?
A: Be honest. It's okay to wrestle with faith. Peace isn't always instant—sometimes it builds, layer by layer. Keep praying. God often changes us before He changes the situation.

Q: Can anxiety be 'prayed away', or do we need more help?
A: Prayer is powerful, but so is wise counsel. If anxiety overwhelms daily life, consider trusted Christian therapy alongside prayer and scripture.

Science & Faith: Why This Works

Brain studies show that interrupting anxious thoughts with calming practices (like prayer, breathing, and reframing) reshapes neural pathways, reducing stress.

God's peace is tangible—Philippians 4:6-7 promises peace that guards both heart and mind. Science aligns with scripture—faith and mental health tools work hand-in-hand.

Positive Reinforcement for Parents

Mum, Dad—when your teen spirals into "what ifs," you now have a roadmap. You're not powerless. With love, prayer, and practice, you can guide them from anxiety to a state of anchored peace.

Even small moments—a whispered scripture, a walk together, a prayer in the car—strengthen their mental resilience.

Dear Parent, this journey is sacred. You're not just raising a child—you're raising a resilient, faith-anchored world-changer. Anxiety doesn't get the final word—God's peace does.

Mother's Teaching #12: Helping Your Teen Swap Anxiety for Faith

A guide for parents from one mother to another—real tools, real prayers, real breakthroughs.

From One Mother to Another…

There was a day I found my daughter curled up under a blanket, tears quietly falling before her chemistry exam. "Mum, what if I fail? What if I just freeze?" she whispered. And that's when I truly *saw* it—anxiety had moved in and made itself at home in her heart.

If you're reading this, you're likely watching your teen wrestle with those same fears. Maybe they don't talk about it much. Maybe they blow it off with "I'm fine." But as mothers, we know better.

Here's how I walked with my teen from anxiety to **faith**—and how you can too.

1. Recognize the Voice of Anxiety

Anxiety sounds like this:

"What if I mess up?"

"They probably don't like me."

"I'm going to fail."

Jesus said in Matthew 6:25, *"Take no thought for your life…"* When our kids take *too many* thoughts, they become anxious. As mums, we need to help them see this isn't just stress—it's an invitation to fight back with **faith**.

2. Today's Triggers: What's Really Stressing Them

We often think it's just the "big stuff" causing anxiety. But for teens today, it's:

- **Academic pressure**: My daughter, Emma, said, "I feel like one bad grade and I'm done."

- **Social media plus FOMO**: Jaden couldn't sleep because he wasn't included in the group chat—and he assumed no one cared.

- **Fear of rejection**: Mia wanted to invite a friend over but said, "What if it's cringe and they say no?"

Anxiety loves to hide in these moments. It feeds off comparison and silence.

3. Jess's Story: The Power of a Prayer Bubble

Jess, a teen we mentored, was melting down before a biology test. Her stomach hurt, her chest was tight. I handed her a notebook and said, "Let's draw it out."

She made two bubbles:

- **Anxiety Bubble** – all the "what-ifs"

- **Prayer Bubble** – a space to give God every fear

Then she prayed:

- "God, this fear is loud—but I choose Your peace."

- "Help me think clearly, not panic."

We practiced breathing:

Inhale: "faith"

Exhale: "fear"

And she walked into that exam steady—not because the test changed, but because **she** did.

4. Tools That Changed Everything
Anxiety-to-Prayer Grid (We filled this out together at the kitchen table)

Trigger

Chemistry exam

Anxious Thought
"I'll fail and embarrass myself."

Prayer
"God, I trust You to help me

Truth Response
Stay calm and think clearly."

Trigger
Being left out of group

Anxious Thought
 "They don't care about me."

Prayer / Truth Response
 "God, remind me I'm loved and not forgotten."

Mindful-Walk Script (We did this one afternoon after school)
- Walk slowly.
- Whisper: *"God, this fear—I give it to You."*
- Breathe in: *"peace."*
- Breathe out: *"panic."*
- Repeat: *"Do not be afraid. I am with you."*

It's simple, but it *works*—our teens need a moment to reset their brain and spirit.

5. Speak Their Language—Without Losing Our Values

To truly connect, I had to learn to speak in a way that landed. When my daughter says, *"I feel this,"* or *"That's so cringe,"* I don't roll my eyes. I listen. I say:

"Let's unpack it together."

"You got this. And God's got you."

6. Parent-Teen Power Prompts That Work

We use these during dinner or even in the car:

"What's something that's bugging you right now?"

"What's your Anxiety Bubble saying?"

"Want to turn that into a Prayer Bubble together?"

Doing the grid together doesn't take more than 10 minutes—but it opens the heart.

7. Why This Isn't Just Emotional—It's Scientific Too

Did you know? According to Jonathan Haidt in *The Anxious Generation*, excessive social media rewires the teen brain—intensifying fear, comparison, and sleeplessness.

Research shows that **prayer** and **mindful breathing** actually calm the brain's fight/flight system. This is not fluff. It's **faith plus neuroscience** working together.

8. This Needs to Be Daily—Not Just When It's Bad

We now follow this simple rhythm:

Morning – "God, I give You my day."

Afternoon – 3-minute reset walk plus breathing.

Evening – Journal one win plus one prayer.

Here's what we added in our Faith Journal:

- Prayer grids
- Verse of the day cards
- Mini reflection pages ("Today, I felt… But God reminded me…")

9. Real Teens. Real Prayers. Real Peace.

Mia's Lunch Prayer:
"God, I feel invisible—but You see me."

She gained courage and texted two classmates, saying, "Hey, I'm here if you ever wanna hang." One replied yes.

Liam's Bedtime Whisper:
"God, my sadness from that mean group chat? It's too big. Your peace is bigger."

He slept better that night.

We don't always fix the situation. But God gives our teens **anxiety-proof peace** that shields their hearts.

10. For Other Parents & Leaders
We now use this with other mums at our church:

Parent-Teen Guides Include:
- Journal prompts to share together
- A "Check-in" sheet (quick: 1–10 scale)
- Discussion questions for small groups or youth nights

For Leaders/Youth Pastors:
- Weekly talk guide: "What was one 'Anxiety Bubble' this week? How did God respond?"

Final Word from This Mum's Heart
Our kids are facing battles we never had to fight—but we have tools, truth, and faith that the world can't offer them.

This isn't about pretending it's all okay. It's about leading our teens to the One who gives **peace that guards their hearts and minds.**

You can do this. One bubble, one prayer, one step at a time.

Swap Anxiety for Faith: A Daily Workbook for Teens & Parents

From the heart of a mother to families walking the journey from fear to faith.

Anxiety-to-Prayer Grid

Truth Response

Use this daily for any situation that causes anxiety, such as tests, social situations, comparisons, or pressure.

Prayer Bubble Activity
Draw two bubbles:

1. **Anxiety Bubble**: Write down all your "what ifs."
2. **Prayer Bubble**: Rewrite each fear as a prayer.

Example:

- Anxiety: "What if I mess up?"
- Prayer: "God, I feel afraid, but I know You strengthen me."

Mindful Walk Script (Use any time of day)
- Stroll for 5 minutes.
- Whisper: "God, this fear—I hand it to You."
- Breathe in: "faith"
- Breathe out: "fear"
- Repeat: "Do not be afraid, for I am with you."

Scripture Prompts for Peace
- "Do not be anxious about anything..." - Philippians 4:6
- "Peace I leave with you; my peace I give you..." - John 14:27

- "Cast all your anxiety on Him..." - 1 Peter 5:7
- "Even though I walk through the valley...I will fear no evil." - Psalm 23:4

Parent & Teen Chat Guide

Weekly Check-In Prompts:
- "What was your biggest anxiety bubble this week?"
- "Did you notice when God gave you peace?"
- "Want to do the prayer grid together for one of your worries?"

Please Leave a Review!

I would be incredibly thankful if you could take just 60 seconds to write a brief review on the platform of purchase, even if it's just a few sentences!

Conclusion:
Keep Showing Up. Keep Trusting God.

Let's be real—there will be tough days. The kind that leaves you feeling exhausted, unsure, maybe even discouraged. However, there will also be moments of profound joy, laughter, and genuine connection that is fulfilling.

Through it all, what your daughter needs most is simple: *you*.

Showing up.

Loving her.

Believing in her.

Pointing her back to God with steady faith and quiet grace.

You won't get it right every time. No one does. But the good news? You don't need to be a perfect parent.

You just need to be a *present* one.

And God will take care of the rest. And with God's help, you're more ready for this than you realize. Be present in every moment because it's in these moments that you're not just shaping but empowering your daughter's future.

You're not just raising a daughter—you're shaping a future woman who will change the world.

Through all the friendship drama, the ups and downs of dating, and family moments that sometimes feel like an emotional rollercoaster, your daughter is growing into the person God created her to be. And right now, she needs you more than ever.

This journey of parenting isn't about having every answer. It's not about controlling her future but preparing her for it. Yes, you'll have those incredible mountaintop moments where everything feels clear and correct. But you'll also face valleys of doubt, frustration, and heartbreak. And through it all—faith in God's plan is what will guide you. He is right there with you every step of the way.

He's given you everything you need:
- His Word to guide you,
- His Spirit to comfort you,
- And His grace to catch you when you stumble.

Think about Jochebed, Moses' mum. She had to let go and trust God to care for what she couldn't control. She didn't just put Moses in a basket—she put him in God's hands. And God didn't let her down. He preserved Moses, protected him, and set him on the path to his destiny.

You're planting those same seeds in your daughter's life—through your prayers, presence, and example.

Remember Sarah? She laughed when God promised her a child in her old age, but faith won over doubt. You might laugh, cry, or wonder if your prayers matter. Keep going. Keep believing.

There will be times, like Lot's wife, when you want to look back—wishing things could go back to when your daughter was little or feeling stuck in regrets. But God's plan is always forward. Don't get caught in fear, guilt, or shame.

Parenting with faith means showing up daily, even when it's hard. It means choosing grace when your daughter makes a mistake. It means teaching her that God is real—not just through Bible verses, but through patience, forgiveness, discipline, and love. You're not just a parent; you're a guide in her faith journey, and your influence is profound.

You're planting seeds that will grow in ways you can't even imagine:
- When you encourage her after a tough day at school.
- When you listen instead of lecture.
- When you stay up late praying instead of stressing.

Your daughter will rise—not because life is perfect, but because she knows who she is. Because she sees in you what it looks like to follow Jesus, even when life is messy. You're not just a parent; you're a shaper of her identity, and your role is integral to it.

So don't underestimate the power of simply showing up—your quiet faith, late-night prayers, sincere apologies, belly laughs, and hugs that say, "You're still loved, no matter what."

Let her see what genuine faith looks like in real life.

Because at the end of the day, it's not about whether she follows every rule perfectly—it's about whether she knows she can always run back to God when she falls. What matters most is that she knows—deep down—that she's deeply loved by you and by her Heavenly Father, whose love is constant, unshakable, and it's a love that doesn't shift with her mood or disappear when she messes up. His love never wavers, rather stable. It's steady and unshakable, even on her most hardest days—no matter what she's feeling or the choices she makes or has to make. Because God's love isn't something she has to earn or strive for. It's already hers. It's already hers. It always has been. She just needs to recognize it, to see it for what it truly is. And once she does, it changes everything.

Final words:
Keep the very act of praying.

Keep showing up.

Keep walking beside her—even when things get messy, confusing, or hard.

You're not alone in this. And neither is she.

And trust God to do what only He can—shaping her heart in ways you can't see.

You're not just raising a daughter.

You''re rasing a woman of faith.

A disciple.

A light in a world that needs it.

A legacy that will last.

God bless you on this journey.

The seeds you plant today will bear fruit for generations to come.

Heartstrings & Heaven

*Simple Heart-to-Heart Conversations
Between a Mother and Her Teenage Daughter*

Introduction (From Me to You)

Dear Mother,

I wrote this book as a mother—just like you—walking the beautiful, complicated, and sacred journey of raising a teenage daughter in today's world.

Simple conversations—sometimes over breakfast, while driving, folding laundry, or right before bed—were the beginning of it all. Not a single script. Just genuine talks, some awkward, some profound, some light. But as time went on, I came to understand that these experiences were profoundly influencing her—not just in terms of conduct, but also in terms of her **heart**.

And in the process... they were shaping **mine**, too.

This book isn't a lecture, and it's not a list of parenting rules or formulas. It's a collection of Spirit-led conversations—many shaped by my own mistakes, my deepening walk with God, and most importantly, the timeless truth of His Word.

I should also mention something very close to my heart—this book wouldn't exist without my daughter. These conversations are not theoretical—they're lived. She is the one I've spoken with, prayed with, cried with, and watched grow. Her journey, her questions, her heart have all helped shape this book. And in a beautiful full-circle moment, **she designed the book cover**, adding her own creative touch to something so personal to us both.

I'm also deeply grateful for all the girls who've come through **TCEC Education Centre** over the years. Their honesty, questions, struggles, and spiritual hunger have added layers of insight and real-life relevance to these pages. What you're reading is not just from one mother to one daughter—but a reflection of many hearts and stories.

If you've ever wondered how to speak truth without sounding preachy... how to guide your daughter without being overbearing... or how to walk with her through the spiritual, emotional, and cultural challenges she's facing—then this is for you.

My prayer is that these simple, Spirit-filled conversations help you both grow—in faith, in obedience, in wisdom, and in love. You don't have to be perfect. You just need to be **present**... and **willing**.

Let the Holy Spirit do the rest.

With love,

Bukky

Mother's Teaching #1: Crushes, Friendships & Obedience to the Holy Spirit

Daughter:
Mum, there's this guy at school... I don't know, I kind of like him. He's nice and makes me laugh.

Mum:
I'm glad you trust me enough to share. You know, I had a crush once too when I was your age. He was tall, charming... and completely not God's plan for me. I didn't ask the Holy Spirit what He thought, and that led to some heartache.

Daughter:
Really?

Mum:
Yes, sweetie, the Holy Spirit lives in you now — and He does speak. But He usually speaks when we're willing to listen and obey. If we ignore Him or go our own way, it gets harder to hear Him clearly.

A real Christian is kind and gentle with others, is honest and careful with how they live, and stays close to God in their heart, even when no one's watching.

Lesson for Mothers:
Use your daughter's emotional openness as a teaching moment. Be honest about your past, not perfect. Help her discern the **voice of God through obedience**. Quote John 10:27: *"My sheep hear my voice, and I know them, and they follow me."*

Mother's Teaching #2: Trends vs. Ancient Paths

Daughter:
Everyone's doing this dance challenge on TikTok. Even the Christian girls.

Mum:
Your generation loves trends — but God's ways aren't trendy. Jeremiah 6:16 says, "Stand at the crossroads and look; ask for the ancient paths... walk in it, and you will find rest."

Daughter:
But it's just fun...

Mum:
I know. But ask yourself: Is it fun that glorifies God? Would Jesus do it with you? The kingdom of God doesn't adapt to trends — it transforms hearts.

Lesson for Mothers:
Expose trends gently. Don't attack. Use Scripture and ask questions to lead your daughter to **conviction**, not just **compliance**. Remind her: the ancient paths aren't outdated — they're eternal.

Mother's Teaching #3: You Need a Strong Spirit

Mum:
Lily, you remember Lucy, your classmate who was bullied and still showed love?

Daughter:
She even said a prayer for them.

Mum:
That's a girl with a strong spirit. Proverbs 18:14 says, "The spirit of a man will sustain his infirmity." Just like your physical body needs food, your spirit needs the Word of God. That's what makes you strong on the inside.

Daughter:
Like gym for my spirit?

Mum:
Exactly. Develop your spirit through prayer, fasting, worship, the Word — because when problems come, it's your spirit that will carry you.

Lesson for Mothers:
Explain spiritual development like **working out** — relatable, real, and requires effort. Use real teen stories to illustrate strength in the spirit. Teach daily spiritual disciplines.

Mother's Teaching #4: Obedience Is Strength

Mum:
When you start recognizing that the Holy Spirit deserves your obedience, strength flows.

Daughter:
So I get stronger by obeying?

Mum:
Yes. Every time you obey a small prompting — like not joining gossip, or praying for someone — your spiritual ears get sharper. You start to grow. You'll begin to perceive God's voice like it says in John 3:3 — "Unless one is born again, he cannot see the kingdom of God."

Lesson for Mothers:

Link **obedience with discernment and strength**. Obedience isn't control — it's God's training ground for maturity. Show daughters that obedience isn't about restriction but **capacity**.

Mother's Teaching #5: Don't Abuse Grace

Mum:
So, you told me you lied to get out of trouble...

Daughter:
I asked God to forgive me though.

Mum:
That's good. But don't keep repeating it because you know God will forgive. Romans 6:1-2 says, "Shall we continue in sin so that grace may abound? God forbid!"

Daughter:
So I shouldn't take forgiveness for granted.

Mum:
Exactly. Grace gives us the strength to overcome sin rather than run away from it.

Lesson for Mothers:
Balance grace and truth. Be firm about **not excusing sin** while still pointing your daughter to the **love of Christ**. "Grace is the system of enablement, not the license for sin."

Mother's Teaching #6: Kingdom Entry is a Choice

Daughter:
Mum, I prayed the salvation prayer last year... so I'm in God's Kingdom, right?

Mum:
Yes, salvation is where it begins — that's the starting point. But remember what Jesus said in Matthew 7:21: "Not everyone who says to me, 'Lord, Lord,' will enter the kingdom of heaven, but only the one who does the will of my Father."

It's not just about saying you believe — it's about living it out. To truly be part of God's kingdom, we need to keep following Him, obeying His ways, and doing what He asks of us.

Daughter:
So it's not just a prayer?

Mum:
It's a surrender — a decision to let God govern your life. Like moving to a new country and living by its rules.

Lesson for Mothers:
Explain **Kingdom citizenship** in terms teens understand: new nationality, new government, new values. Use analogies like **moving countries** or **changing schools**.

Mother's Teaching #7: Burn With God's Flame

Mum:
Joseph lost his coat of many colours, but he didn't lose his fire. The fire of God was still burning in him.

Daughter:
Like being hurt but not quitting?

Mum:
Yes. Even if people take things from you — your friends, your reputation — keep the fire of God burning. Feed it with the Word, worship, prayer.

Lesson for Mothers:
Show your daughters how **pain doesn't extinguish the fire**, but feeds it. Teach them how **to process pain spiritually** and grow through it.

Mother's Teaching #8: The Will of God Is the Platform

Mum:
Your classroom, your social media, your gift — they're platforms to serve God.

Daughter:
Like Peter's boat?

Mum:
Exactly. Luke 5:3 says Jesus used Peter's boat as a platform to teach the crowd. What's your platform today?

Lesson for Mothers:
Help your daughter identify her **"boat"** — and use it for God's purpose. Whether it's a talent, classroom, or online voice — it's a kingdom tool.

Mother's Teaching #9: Don't Give Satan the Keys

Mum:
When you disobey, you hand the keys of your life to Satan. Just like Adam did. Jesus had die to go to hell, rise from death and take them back.

Daughter:
So every choice is serious.

Mum:
Yes, God won't force you — it's your choice. That's what makes it worship: when you choose Him. Like when you say no to something tempting, like a party that doesn't feel right, or when you choose to pray instead — that's you giving God the keys to your life.

But if you hand those keys to the enemy, he won't hold back. He'll use them to take control. That's what happened with Adam — he gave the enemy access, and it cost him the garden.

God wants to lead you, but you have to let Him.

Lesson for Mothers:
Use real-life examples to show how choices unlock spiritual consequences. Teach about **authority**, **legal access**, and how obedience keeps God on the throne of your heart.

Mother's Teaching #10: Be a Path Maker

Mum:
Did you know David was the youngest, but still became king? He was a path maker.

Daughter:
So I can be one too?

Mum:
Yes. Maybe no one in our family has ever gone that far, but you can be the one to break the limit. Like Deborah, Josiah, or Esther.

Lesson for Mothers:
Stir **prophetic identity** in your daughter. Give her vision beyond your generation. Speak boldly: *"You are a path maker."*

Mother's Teaching #11: Discipline is the Path to Transformation

Daughter: Mum, why is it so hard to change? I keep falling back into old habits.

Mum: Because change isn't just desire, it's discipline. You can't transform without it.

"You don't transform if you cannot be disciplined."

Mum: Think of Daniel. He was a teenager in Babylon, surrounded by temptation. But he *purposed in his heart* not to defile himself (Daniel 1:8). That was discipline. It takes small, consistent decisions to stay aligned with God.

Lesson for Mothers:
- Help your daughter **set small, spiritual routines** (prayer, fasting, boundaries).
- Explain that **discipline is not punishment**, it's how the Spirit shapes her into a woman of purpose.

Mother's Teaching #12: Steadfastness is Your Access Pass

"The passcode to the realm of God is continuing." — (based on Acts 2:42)

Mum: Sweetheart, I know it feels like no one is as serious as you about God. But don't stop. God is watching your consistency. God. But don't stop. God is watching your consistency.

Daughter: Even when I feel alone?

Mum: Especially then. The disciples continued *steadfastly*, and that's when the power came (Acts 2:42). Your strength isn't in popularity, it's in perseverance.

Lesson for Mothers:
- Reinforce that **faithfulness is noticed by heaven** even when ignored on earth.
- Encourage her with real stories (e.g. a teen who kept attending fellowship alone).

Mother's Teaching #13: Knowledge Isn't Yours Until You Comprehend It

Mum: Baby girl, you've read that verse many times, but has it entered your heart?

Daughter: What do you mean?

Mum: It's not yours until you comprehend it. Reading about wisdom is different from walking in it. Like you study math until it makes sense—do the same with God's word.

"What you have not comprehended is not yours."

Lesson for Mothers:
- Teach daughters to **meditate, not just memorize.**
- Encourage journaling or voice notes after reading scripture to track understanding.

Mother's Teaching #14: **The Spirit Sustains Your Infirmity**

Mum: Remember Lily who tried to lift her grandmother but couldn't?

Daughter: Yes, she cried and felt helpless.

Mum: That's what happens when you don't grow your spirit. Proverbs 18:14 says *"The spirit of a man will sustain his infirmity."* If your spirit is weak, you collapse under pressure.

Lesson for Mothers:
- Help daughters understand the **importance of growing their spirit** like they grow academically or physically.
- Prioritize spiritual disciplines like prayer, solitude, and worship.

Mother's Teaching #15: The Wounded Spirit is Satan's Target

Mum: You know why the devil tries to wound your heart with betrayal, heartbreak, and shame?

Daughter: Why?

Mum: Because your spirit is where your strength comes from. If he wounds it, you'll feel empty. *"A wounded spirit who can bear?"* (Proverbs 18:14)

Lesson for Mothers:
- Normalize **emotional healing as spiritual warfare**.
- Teach daughters to bring their pain to God—not social media, music, or boys.

Mother's Teaching #16: Repentance Is Like Updating Your Phone

Mum: How often do you update your phone?

Daughter: All the time. New features, bug fixes...

Mum: That's repentance. It's not just saying sorry. It's an update to align with God's latest instruction in your life.

"Repentance is a continuous thing. When you perceive God's perspective, you must adjust."

Lesson for Mothers:
- Repentance isn't about shame but **realignment.**
- Teach daughters to love correction and see it as growth, not guilt.

Mother's Teaching #17: You Were Born into a New Kingdom

Daughter: Sometimes I don't feel like I belong anywhere.

Mum: That's because your nationality changed when you gave your life to Jesus.

"Once you're born again, your nationality is heaven."

Mum: You're not just a British, American, Ghanaian—you're a citizen of heaven (Philippians 3:20). That means you follow heaven's laws, not earthly trends.

Lesson for Mothers:
- Reaffirm your daughter's **heavenly identity.**
- Teach her that **living differently is normal** for Kingdom teens.

Mother's Teaching #18: You Have Legal Access to the Holy Spirit

Mum: Just like Adam gave the devil access through disobedience, you give access through your choices.

"The cross is a legal declaration. When you believe it, the Holy Spirit has access to you."

Daughter: So I decide who enters my life—God or the enemy?

Mum: Exactly. Obedience is a door. That's why Satan tempts you—he wants legal ground. But the cross gave Jesus the key back. Stay under His governance.

Lesson for Mothers:
- Explain **legal access in spiritual terms**—authority, access, and protection.
- Show her how obedience is her spiritual **yes or no** to different spirits.

Mother's Teaching #19: Don't Copy Peter—Find Your Own Word

Mum: You remember how Peter walked on water?

Daughter: Yeah, that was powerful.

Mum: But only because Jesus told him to. Some girls read that story, tried to walk on water—and drowned. Because it wasn't their word.

Daughter: That's scary.

Mum: The Bible is for everyone, but you must wait for the Holy Spirit to apply it to your life. Don't copy, wait for revelation.

Lesson for Mothers:
- Teach your daughter to **wait for personal revelation**.
- Encourage her to ask: "Lord, what are You saying to me *now*?"

Mother's Teaching #20: The Holy Spirit Is Hoping You'll Choose Him

Mum: The Holy Spirit is a gentleman. He won't force you. He stands by, hoping you'll choose to follow Him.

"It's not worship if God is the only option. It's worship when you have many and still choose Him."

Daughter: So, every time I choose Him, I'm worshiping?

Mum: Yes. That's the kind of person God governs—a girl who chooses His will even when it costs.

Lesson for Mothers:
- Model this with your own choices: "Today, I wanted to do X, but I chose God."
- Teach her that **obedience is worship**, and worship is voluntary.

Mother's Teachings #21: The Power of Repentance and Daily Adjustment

Daughter: Why, Mom, do you continuously insist that even after I surrendered my life to Jesus, I must continue to repent?

Mother: Sweetheart, repentance isn't just a one-time thing. When Jesus preached, His first message was "Repent, for the kingdom of heaven is at hand." (Matthew 4:17). The kingdom is here, but it means you must keep making adjustments in your life to align with God's will. It's like updating your apps on your phone — you wouldn't want to miss the latest version, right?

Daughter: So repentance is like fixing what's wrong and keeping my life "updated" spiritually?

Mother: Exactly! Every time you perceive God's perspective differently, you adjust your heart and actions. This is how you grow and stay in His kingdom.

Mother's Teachings #22: Hearing and Obeying the Holy Spirit

Mother: Do you know why some people say they don't hear God?

Daughter: No, why?

Mother: Because the Holy Spirit speaks to those who obey Him. When you start obeying His promptings, you become stronger spiritually, and hearing His voice becomes clearer. (John 14:26) If you're not hearing, maybe you're not obeying fully.

Daughter: So obedience opens the door for God to speak?

Mother: Indeed, the secret to obtaining God's direction is obedience.

Mother's Teachings #23: Discipline is Essential for Transformation

Daughter: Sometimes I find it hard to be disciplined in my spiritual life.

Mother: I understand. But remember, without discipline, there's no transformation. The Bible says, "No discipline seems pleasant at the time, but painful. However, for those who have been trained by it, it later yields a harvest of righteousness and tranquility. Hebrews 12:11.

Think of David; he trained himself to follow God even when it was hard, and God made him a man after His own heart.

Daughter: So discipline shapes who I become?

Mother: Yes, it builds the muscles of your spirit.

Mother's Teachings #24: God's Ancient Ways Cannot Be Edited

Mother: Your generation loves trends, right?

Daughter: Yeah, I like what's popular.

Mother: That's typical, but God's methods are timeless and ageless. (Psalm 119:89) They can't be "edited" or updated like trends. You need to root your life in God's eternal Word, not temporary patterns.

Daughter: So I shouldn't follow what everyone else is doing?

Mother: Exactly. Be rooted in God, not the latest fad.

Mother's Teachings #25: Kingdom Entrance is By Regeneration

Daughter: What does it mean to enter the kingdom of heaven?

Mother: It means being born again — a new birth. Jesus said in John 3:3, "Unless one is born again, he cannot see the kingdom of God." It's not about being good; it's about a spiritual transformation where you receive new life from God.

Daughter: So just believing in Jesus changes everything?

Mother: Yes! That's how you get a new spiritual nationality — you become a citizen of heaven.

Mother's Teachings #26: The Importance of Intellectual Understanding and the Holy Spirit

Mother: The Bible says God's ways require wisdom, which we don't naturally have. That's why the Holy Spirit helps us understand scripture and apply it. (1 Corinthians 2:14)

Daughter: Like when I don't get something I read?

Mother: Exactly! Pray and ask the Holy Spirit to teach you. For example, if you read about Peter walking on water but try it without God's help, it will be dangerous. The Holy Spirit helps you know when and how to apply God's Word safely.

Mother's Teachings #27: Living God's Will in Every Role

Mother: Whatever job or role you have — student, musician, athlete — it's your platform to serve God.

Daughter: Even if I'm just a student?

Mother: Yes! Jesus used Peter's boat as a platform to minister. Your classroom, your social media, your friendships — all can be tools for God's kingdom.

Mother's Teachings #28: The Choice to Obey God

Daughter: Does God force us to obey Him?

Mother: No, He gives us the choice. God doesn't want robots. True worship is choosing Him when you have many options.

Daughter: So obedience is a decision I make?

Mother: Yes, and your life becomes a "God option" when you choose to obey Him consistently.

Mother's Teachings #29: Obedience Leads to Greatness in the Kingdom

Mother: Jesus said in Matthew 5:19, "Whoever obeys and teaches these commandments will be called great in the kingdom of heaven." Obedience brings blessing and favor.

Daughter: So obeying God makes me great?

Mother: Yes, and God gives you gifts to serve His purpose, whether as a teacher, writer, or prophet. You grow as you faithfully serve.

Mother's Teachings #30: Learning from Adam's Mistake

Mother: Remember Adam? God told him not to eat from the tree of knowledge of good and evil. He chose to disobey, and sin entered the world. (Genesis 2:16-17)

Daughter: But Eve was there too.

Mother: Yes, but Adam was responsible because he heard God directly. We must stand on God's Word, even when tempted, just like Adam should have.

Mother's Teaching #31: Kingdom Rules Apply Only to Kingdom Citizens

Daughter: Mom, why do we have to follow God's rules, but my friend who isn't a Christian doesn't?

Mother: Think about it like this: when you live in a country, you follow its laws, but when you visit another, you obey theirs. God's rules are for those who have entered His kingdom by faith. If you're a citizen of His kingdom, you obey His commands because you've given Him permission to lead your life.

Mother's Teaching #32: Faithfulness Brings Added Responsibility

Mother: God blesses those who are faithful with what He's given them. Like a teacher who also becomes a writer — God adds more gifts and opportunities as you prove faithful.

Daughter: So I need to be faithful in little things?

Mother: Yes, just like the parable of the talents (Matthew 25:21). Being faithful in what you have leads to greater responsibilities.

Mother's Teaching #33: God is Gathering an Army for His Purpose

Mother: The Bible talks about God raising an army for His day of judgment (Joel 2:1-11). You, my daughter, are part of that army if you choose to serve Him faithfully.

Daughter: What kind of army is that?

Mother: It's a spiritual army made up of individuals dedicated to God's will who shine His light in a world full of darkness.

Mother's Teaching #34: Don't Abuse God's Grace

Daughter: Mom, can I continue to do evil even if God pardons my sins?

Mother: No, dear. Paul says in Romans 6:1-2, "Shall we go on sinning so that grace may increase? By no means!" Grace is not a license to sin; it's the power to live right.

Mother's Teaching #35: Let God's Flame Burn Away Your Pain

Mother: Just like Joseph's coat was taken away, God's flame burned away his pain and made him stronger (Genesis 37-50).

Daughter: How does that help me?

Mother: If someone hurt you, let God's flame heal your heart, so bitterness doesn't control you.

Mother's Teaching #36: Your Light Challenges Darkness

Mother: When your light burns bright with God's Word, it pushes away darkness around you. (Matthew 5:16)

Daughter: So I can be a light in my school and community?

Mother: Yes! Keep feeding your fire with God's Word daily.

Mother's Teaching #37: Be a Path-Maker, Not Just a Path-Finder

Mother: You don't have to follow the same path as everyone before you. Be a path-maker — someone who breaks barriers and creates new paths for others to follow.

Daughter: Like who?

Mother: Think of Esther who risked everything to save her people. Today, you can be that young person who changes your environment with God's power.

Mother's Teaching #38: Comprehension Makes God's Word Yours

Mother: You can read the Bible, but until you truly understand it, it's not yours. It's like having a key but not knowing how to use it.

Daughter: So I need to ask God to help me understand?

Mother: Yes, ask the Holy Spirit to reveal the meaning and make it real in your life.

Mother's Teaching #39: Spiritual Growth Requires Persistence

Mother: The disciples kept following Jesus even when no one else did. Growth comes when you continue faithfully, even when it looks "stupid" or lonely.

Daughter: That's hard sometimes.

Mother: I know, but ask God to give you a heart that never gives up.

Mother's Teaching #40: Protect Your Heart as Your Spiritual Altar

Mother: Your heart is like an altar where God dwells. Protect it by rejoicing, praying, and guarding your thoughts (Philippians 4:7-8).

Daughter: How do I protect it?

Mother: Keep your heart fixed on God, be grateful, and stay away from things that make you unhappy.

Mother's Teaching #41: Loving God Means Obeying Him

Daughter: How can I know I genuinely love God, Mom?

Mother: It's not just about saying it, sweetheart. Jesus said, *"If you love Me, you will keep My commandments."* (John 14:15)

Daughter: So, love is more than just feelings?

Mother: Exactly. Real love is obedience. You obey God not out of fear, but because you love Him.

Mother's Teaching #42: Your Purpose Is to Love

Mother: People often search for their purpose, but Jesus already told us.

Daughter: Really? What is it?

Mother: Love God. Love others. That's it. (Matthew 22:37-39) As you do this daily, you're walking in your purpose.

Mother's Teaching #43: Love Flows Like a River

Mother: When you love God sincerely, love will begin to overflow from your life like a river.

Daughter: What does that mean?

Mother: It means you'll naturally be kind, forgiving, generous, and thoughtful — not by force, but because you're filled with God's love.

Mother's Teaching #44: Love Is a Cheerful Sacrifice

Daughter: Why does love feel so hard sometimes?

Mother: Because real love is a **sacrifice**, and it often costs something. But the kind of love Jesus taught us is cheerful — it gives even when it's not convenient.

Mother's Teaching #45: Love Takes Time and Effort

Mother: Love isn't a quick text or a cute emoji. It's time. It's effort. It's patience.

Daughter: So, love can be tiring?

Mother: Sometimes, yes. But it's always worth it. Just like Jesus patiently loved us. (1 Corinthians 13)

Mother's Teaching #46: Love Is Your New Identity

Daughter: People at school act like love is weakness.

Mother: That's the world's idea. In God's kingdom, love is strength. Jesus said, *"By this all will know you are My disciples, if you love one another."* (John 13:35)

Mother's Teaching #47: You Can't Heal What You Carry

Mother: If you carry the same sin as the land, you can't heal the land.

Daughter: What do you mean?

Mother: Think of Lot's wife. She couldn't let go of Sodom, so she couldn't survive it. (Genesis 19:26) God needs people who are set apart — not entangled.

Mother's Teaching #48: Be a Nazirite in Your Generation

Daughter: What's a Nazirite?

Mother: Someone completely set apart for God. Like Samson or John the Baptist. If you want to change your generation, you can't blend in. You have to stand out — in purity, purpose, and obedience.

Mother's Teaching #49: God's Voice Is Greater Than Your Mind

Daughter: Sometimes I don't get what God wants me to do.

Mother: That's okay. God's thoughts are higher than ours. He speaks with an intellect we can't reach without the Holy Spirit.

Daughter: So, how can I understand?

Mother: Through obedience. Once you obey, then understanding comes. Proverbs 3:5 says, *"Trust in the Lord with all your heart and lean not on your own understanding."*

Mother's Teaching #50: Obey Even If It Doesn't Make Sense

Mother: If you tell a cat you're going for an exam, it won't understand.

Daughter: (laughs) Of course not.

Mother: That's how we are with God sometimes. We won't always *get it* — it might not make sense to us in the moment. But He asks us to trust and obey anyway. And once we do, He often shows us *why* later on.

Remember what Jesus said:

> *"If anyone chooses to do God's will, he will find out whether my teaching comes from God or whether I speak on my own."*
> — **(John 7:17, NIV)**

In simpler terms, Jesus is saying: *You'll understand the truth once you obey.* In other words, *you'll know after you've done it.*

Mother's Teaching #51: You Cannot Change What You Secretly Agree With

Daughter: Why do I still struggle with the same things in my generation?

Mother: Because sometimes we carry the same weakness as the land we're trying to fix. You can't change what you're secretly in agreement with.

Daughter: So what should I do?

Mother: Be separated like Daniel—he lived in Babylon but didn't become Babylon. (Daniel 1:8)

Mother's Teaching #52: Your Spirit Is Designed to Carry Weight

Daughter: Why do some things feel too heavy to handle?

Mother: Because your strength is not in your muscles—it's in your spirit. *"The spirit of a man will sustain his infirmity."* (Proverbs 18:14)

Daughter: So my spirit needs to be strong?

Mother: Yes. Like going to school to grow your mind, you must feed your spirit daily with prayer, the Word, and obedience.

Mother's Teaching #53: Don't Give the Devil Your Keys

Mother: When Adam sinned, he handed over the authority God gave him to Satan—like giving the devil the keys to his house.

Daughter: That's scary.

Mother: Yes. Disobedience still does that today. Guard your decisions, because your choices can either give access to the Holy Spirit or the enemy.

Mother's Teaching #54: God Can Only Govern Where He Is Welcome

Daughter: Why does God feel far sometimes?

Mother: Because God governs by permission. If you don't welcome Him, He won't force you. That's why Jesus said, *"I stand at the door and knock..."* (Revelation 3:20)

Daughter: So He only rules where He's invited?

Mother: Yes, that's kingdom life. You must *let Him lead.*

Mother's Teaching #55: Gifts Grow When You Use Them Faithfully

Mother: God gives gifts based on your assignment. But He adds more when you are faithful.

Daughter: Like how?

Mother: If you're a teacher and you teach faithfully, God may add writing, counseling, or influence—just like He added writing to Ben.

Daughter: So I just need to start with what I have?

Mother: Yes. Use what's in your hand. (Matthew 25:21)

Mother's Teaching #56: Your Platform Is God's Stage

Mother: Your classroom, your phone, your online presence—they're all platforms.

Daughter: Platforms for what?

Mother: For Jesus. Just like Peter lent his boat to Jesus for preaching, you must let Jesus use your life as a platform. (Luke 5:3)

Mother's Teaching #57: Obedience Unlocks Expression

Daughter: Why don't I hear God clearly?

Mother: Maybe because you're not obeying what He already said. The Holy Spirit speaks, but obedience unlocks more expression.

Daughter: So obedience makes me more sensitive?

Mother: Exactly. The more you obey, the clearer He becomes.

Mother's Teaching #58: You Are Not a Robot—You Choose to Worship

Mother: God didn't make you a robot.

Daughter: What do you mean?

Mother: Worship is a choice. It's only real when you have other options but you still choose God. That's what makes it powerful.

Daughter: So choosing God in a crowd that doesn't is real worship?

Mother: Yes. That's kingdom life.

Mother's Teaching #59: Don't Abuse Grace

Daughter: But God will forgive me, right?

Mother: Yes, but Paul says, *"Shall we continue in sin that grace may abound? God forbid!"* (Romans 6:1)

Daughter: So I shouldn't take God's grace for granted?

Mother: No. Grace is not a license to sin. It's strength to overcome it.

Mother's Teaching #60: Keep the Flame Burning

Mother: Joseph's brothers took his coat, but they couldn't take the flame inside him.

Daughter: What flame?

Mother: His inner fire for God. That's what kept him through betrayal, prison, and promotion. (Genesis 39)

Daughter: How do I keep mine burning?

Mother: Add wood every day—prayer, the Word, obedience. Don't let the fire die.

Mother's Teaching #61: Repentance Is a Lifestyle

Daughter: Mom, I already gave my life to Jesus. Why do I need to keep repenting?

Mother: Because repentance isn't just for when you got saved. It's a way of life. Every time you perceive God's view, you adjust. That's what it means to walk with Him.

Daughter: So it's like making updates?

Mother: Yes, just like you update your apps—your life needs to update when God reveals a new truth.

Mother's Teaching #62: Real Transformation Requires Discipline

Daughter: I want to change, but it feels too hard sometimes.

Mother: That's because true transformation requires discipline. You don't grow by wishing. You grow by choosing.

Daughter: Even when I don't feel like it?

Mother: Especially then. Jesus said, *"Take up your cross daily."* (Luke 9:23) That's not always easy, but it's always worth it.

Mother's Teaching #63: You're Born Into a New Nation

Mother: When you gave your life to Jesus, you didn't just join a church—you became a citizen of heaven.

Daughter: What does that mean?

Mother: It means heaven is your home country now. And like any nation, it has laws, values, and culture that shape how you live.

Daughter: So I should live by kingdom standards?

Mother: Exactly. (Philippians 3:20)

Mother's Teaching #64: Your Life Must Be the "God Option"

Mother: When your friends are making choices, can they look at your life and say, "That's what God would want"?

Daughter: I hope so.

Mother: That's what it means for your life to be the "God option"—you live in a way that reflects His will even when others don't.

Mother's Teaching #65: A Healthy Spirit Makes You Strong

Daughter: I felt so helpless during that challenge.

Mother: That's a sign your spirit needs to grow. Remember Proverbs 18:14? *"The spirit of a man will sustain his infirmity."* If your spirit is strong, you'll carry what others break under.

Mother's Teaching #66: You Can't Borrow Spiritual Strength

Mother: Lily tried to carry her sick grandma but couldn't because she didn't have the strength.

Daughter: But she tried really hard.

Mother: Yes, but strength must be built before the crisis. Spiritually too—you can't borrow fire when the test comes. You must already be burning.

Mother's Teaching #67: What You Comprehend Becomes Yours

Daughter: I read the Bible, but I don't always understand it.

Mother: That's okay. Ask the Holy Spirit to help you. And keep praying about it until it becomes real to you.

Daughter: So I shouldn't just read and move on?

Mother: No. What you haven't *comprehended* isn't yours yet. You must pray the Word into your heart until it becomes part of you.

Mother's Teaching #68: Your Calling Shouldn't Be Eclipsed

Mother: The world wants to hide your light and shut your voice. But Isaiah 60:1 says, *"Arise, shine, for your light has come."*

Daughter: So I should stand out?

Mother: Yes. Don't let your calling be eclipsed. In your school, on your phone, in your dreams—be radiant.

Mother's Teaching #69: You're a Path-Maker, Not Just a

Follower
Mother: You can be the first to do something godly in your family, your school, or your community.

Daughter: But no one else has done it before.

Mother: That's exactly why God called you. Gideon was hiding, yet God said, *"Go in this thy might."* (Judges 6:14) Be a path-maker. Don't wait for someone else to lead.

Mother's Teaching #70: You Have Two Voices Competing—Choose the Holy Spirit

Daughter: Sometimes I feel pulled in two directions.

Mother: That's because two voices are always speaking—the Holy Spirit and the enemy.

Daughter: How do I know which one to follow?

Mother: Check the fruit. The Holy Spirit will always lead you toward truth, love, and purpose. The enemy pulls you toward fear, disobedience, and confusion. Choose the voice that aligns with God's Word.

Conclusion (A Final Word from My Heart)

Dear Daughter,

As you've walked through these conversations, I pray you've seen that being a teen girl who follows Jesus is not strange—it's powerful.

You don't have to wait until you're older to obey God, hear His voice, or be used by Him. **You are already part of His plan.**

Your identity is not found in social media, trends, or people's approval. It's found in the One who created you, saved you, and filled you with His Spirit. Loving God isn't just a feeling—it's a lifestyle of obedience. And loving others is how that obedience becomes visible.

You were made to reflect Jesus. To burn with holy fire. To walk in truth and power.

You were born for this generation—but not to be like it. **You are set apart.**

To every mother reading this—thank you. Thank you for choosing to disciple your daughter when it would have been easier to be silent. Thank you for sowing truth in a culture of compromise. **God sees you. And so does your daughter.**

Keep the conversations going.

Keep the hearts connected.

Keep heaven involved.

Let your life, and your daughter's, be a beautiful echo of obedience and love—the kind that reaches from earth to heaven... and back again.

If this book has blessed you in any way, I warmly invite you to **share it with another mother or daughter** who may need encouragement too. Post the link, recommend it in your circles, and please take a moment to **leave a review**—I'll read every single one. Your words will help me grow and may help someone else find just what they need in these pages.

With all my heart,
Bukky

Other Books You'll Love!

1. The Fear of The Lord: How God's Honour Guarantees Your Peace

2. Parenting Teenage Boys for Purpose: Guiding Godly Young Men to Walk in Charisma, Character, Calling, Life Skills, and Christ-Centered Confidence

3. Raising Teenagers to Choose Wisely: Keeping your Teen Secure in a Big World

4. Spelling one: An Interactive Vocabulary & Spelling Workbook for 5-Year-Olds. *(With Audiobook Lessons)*

5. Spelling Two: An Interactive Vocabulary & Spelling Workbook for 6-Year-Olds. *(With Audiobook Lessons)*

6. Spelling Three: An Interactive Vocabulary & Spelling Workbook for 7-Year-Olds. *(With Audiobook Lessons)*

7. Spelling Four: An Interactive Vocabulary & Spelling Workbook for 8-Year-Olds. *(With Audiobook Lessons)*

8. Spelling Five: An Interactive Vocabulary & Spelling Workbook for 9-Year-Olds. *(With Audiobook Lessons)*

9. Spelling Six: An Interactive Vocabulary & Spelling Workbook for 10 & 11 Years Old. *(With Audiobook Lessons)*

10. Spelling Seven: An Interactive Vocabulary & Spelling Workbook for 12-14 Years-Old. *(With Audiobook Lessons)*

11. [Raising Boys in Today's Digital World: Proven Positive Parenting Tips for Raising Respectful, Successful, and Confident Boys](#)

12. [Raising Girls in Today's Digital World: Proven Positive Parenting Tips for Raising Respectful, Successful, and Confident Girls](#)

13. [Raising Kids in Today's Digital World: Proven Positive Parenting Tips for Raising Respectful, Successful, and Confident Kids](#)

14. [The Child Development and Positive Parenting Master Class 2-in-1 Bundle: Proven Methods for Raising Well-Behaved and Intelligent Children, with Accelerated Learning Methods](#)

15. [Parenting Teens in Today's Challenging World 2-in-1 Bundle: Proven Methods for Improving Teenager's Behaviour with Positive Parenting and Family Communication](#)

16. [Life Strategies for Teenagers: Positive Parenting, Tips and Understanding Teens for Better Communication and a Happy Family](#)

17. [Parenting Teen Girls in Today's Challenging World: Proven Methods for Improving Teenager's Behaviour with Whole Brain Training](#)

18. [Parenting Teen Boys in Today's Challenging World: Proven Methods for Improving Teenager's Behaviour with Whole Brain Training](#)

19. [101 Tips For Helping With Your Child's Learning: Proven Strategies for Accelerated Learning and Raising Smart Children Using Positive Parenting Skills](#)

20. <u>101 Tips for Child Development: Proven Methods for Raising Children and Improving Kids Behavior with Whole Brain Training</u>

21. <u>Financial Tips to Help Kids: Proven Methods for Teaching Kids Money Management and Financial Responsibility</u>

22. <u>Healthy Habits for Kids: Positive Parenting Tips for Fun Kids Exercises, Healthy Snacks, and Improved Kids Nutrition</u>

23. <u>Mini Habits for Happy Kids: Proven Parenting Tips for Positive Discipline and Improving Kids' Behavior</u>

24. <u>Good Habits for Healthy Kids 2-in-1 Combo Pack: Proven Positive Parenting Tips for Improving Kid's Fitness and Children's Behavior</u>

25. <u>T Raising Teenagers to Choose Wisely: Keeping your Teen Secure in a Big World</u>

26. <u>Tips for #CollegeLife: Powerful College Advice for Excelling as a College Freshman</u>

27. <u>The Career Success Formula: Proven Career Development Advice and Finding Rewarding Employment for Young Adults and College Graduates</u>

28. <u>The Motivated Young Adult's Guide to Career Success and Adulthood: Proven Tips for Becoming a Mature Adult, Starting a Rewarding Career, and Finding Life Balance</u>

29. <u>Bedtime Stories for Kids: Short Funny Stories and poems Collection for Children and Toddlers</u>

30. Bedtime Stories for Kids: More Adventures in Healthy Living Fun and Faith-Filled Stories to Grow Kindness, Courage, and Care

31. [Bedtime Stories for Kids Faith and Fun Stories 50 Delightful Tales of Joy, Hope, and Heartfelt Lessons](#)

32. [Guide for Boarding School Life](#)

Your Free Gift!

As a way of saying thank you for Your purchase, I have included a gift that you can download at <u>TCEC publishing .com</u>

References

1. **Bible Verses About Being True to Yourself**
2. A thoughtful collection of scripture encouraging authenticity and faithfulness to who God created you to be.
3. **Career Guidance and Life Purpose**
4. For advice on career and calling, explore helpful articles at Brain Storm International.
5. **The Book of John — Words of Jesus (NIV)**
6. Dive into chapter 7 of John's gospel and reflect on the teachings of Jesus.
7. **King, W. (2024)**
8. *"Grace, Music, and Second Chances at York County Jail"* in *American Jails* reminds us of hope and redemption in unexpected places. American Jails, 38(1), 25-27.
9. **Proverbs 13:20 — Wisdom in Friendship**
10. "Walk with the wise and become wise, for a companion of fools suffers harm." A gentle reminder about the company we keep. See the verse here: bibleapps.com

11. **Peace that Transcends Understanding** (2021)

12. This is an inspiring reminder from *the Florida Times Union* about how God's peace protects our hearts and minds in Christ Jesus (A-8).

13. **The Grace of God to Overcome Worldly Passions** (2022)

14. From *Florida Times-Union*, a passage encouraging us to embrace God's grace to live godly and self-controlled lives (B-6).

15. **Washington, J. (2015).**

16. *"Drop and give me 20"* — A call to discipline and perseverance featured in *The Triangle Tribune*, 16(6), 6B.

17. **How to Overcome Temptation**

18. Practical guidance rooted in faith to help parents and families navigate life's challenges.

19. **You Never Know How God is Working in People's Lives — Princess' Story**

20. A powerful testimony of God's quiet work in everyday lives.

www.ingramcontent.com/pod-product-compliance
Lightning Source LLC
Chambersburg PA
CBHW052029070526
44584CB00016B/1965